LASTING

Intimate Secrets

Loving,

Passionate

Endeavors!

Lasting Intimate Secrets!

www.BlueSunRomance.com

Blue Sun Romance gladly donates a percentage of proceeds
from this book to help Spinal Cord Injury Research through
The Christopher and Dana Reeve Foundation.
Go Forward!

Reprint, production, and permission queries, as well as Comments, affiliations, and translations may be addressed to:

Blue Sun Productions, Inc.
btdormire@gmail.com

Acknowledgments

For permission to use the selections reprinted in this pamphlet, the authors are grateful to the following publishers and copyright holders:

1. CROWN PUBLISHERS, INC. From the JOY OF SEX by Alex Comfort. Reprinted by permission of Crown Publishers, Inc. Copyright © 1986 by Mitchell Beazley Publishers.
2. IStockphotos, by Getty Images. www.istockphotos.com
3. B. T. Dormire photo images, Copyright © Blue Sun Productions, Inc.

Artistic Production

1. Print Interior Formatting & Design by the crew at 52 Novels. www.52novels.com
2. Front & Back Cover Design, EBook Cover Design. www.ebooklaunch.com

Reader Discretion Advised

~

LASTING

Intimate Secrets...

Loving, Passionate Endeavors!
The Owner's Manual for Romantic
Couples.

Written By,
William &
Dionna
Jorgensen
Leiksa, Finland

Edited By,
B.T. Dormire

Blue Sun Productions, LLC
Colorado Springs, CO

www.Bluesunromance.com

Table of Contents

INTRODUCTION

LASTING INTIMATE SECRETS

Lasting Intimate Secrets establishes a loving foundation for couples longing to be more than just casual romantics with their 'significant other'. Written in three parts, **Lasting Intimate Secrets, Great Letters of Passion,** and **Poemas De Amor (Love Poems),** authors **William** and **Dionna Jorgensen,** and **Juan Francisco Ladero** have compiled this simple yet relatable book to sustain the romantic insight and compassion required of any long term, ever-budding relationship.

To avoid the myths and hype that surround the openness of today's sexually dominated culture, people would much rather enjoy great physical love, while also understanding each other's quirks, needs, and passions. The promotion of in-fashion romance and the ability to hold together stable, companion-based feelings, all stem from engaging interactions, and healthy, loving endeavors. These are the emotional and physical needs we hope we receive from the men or women in our lives.

Many readers find varying degrees of help from scores of suggestive books on intimacy and love. The point of writing *Lasting Intimate Secrets*, is to direct couples toward overcoming their perceived physical and emotional limitations. By knowing how to extend and skillfully enhance intimate abilities, couples can thrive on pleasing their partner to exhaustion with loving, physical attention.

It is not difficult to acquire a comprehensive talent at being a good lover. Staying one challenges us to remember the basics of friendship, respect, tenderness, and imaginative kindnesses thrown in as a routine practice.

The Jorgensens underline varying examples of improving physical intimacy and individual performance. They consider the benefits of appreciating one's partner, ways to improve one's physical stamina for long term, devoted passion, and how to nurture these aspects toward mutually emotional gains.

Physical intimacy is the great bond that keeps people loving and connected to each other.

Desiring the playful, heartfelt affections that come with such a harmonious tie, intimacy can also suggest what constitutes a lasting, cohesive relationship between a man and a woman.

LASTING INTIMATE SECRETS builds upon the sparks of your initial and ever renewable attraction to someone. It helps you enjoy the smiling pass along a beach with a handsome stranger, or jostling by a fellow romantic in the grocery aisles of your neighborhood store. You could be anywhere eyeing a beautiful, gorgeous haired partner with whom you could love for a very long time. And who knows? They might even feel the same!

The suggestions you're about to uncover strive to fulfill two very significant human needs. The first – and in many people's everyday thoughts is **'*Sexual Gratification'** – the loving promise one person makes of their body to another, filled with inspiration and daring, and the need to have such a thing in one's life returned.

The second, is the overpowering human **'*Need to Feel Important'**. This nurturing aspect of life shows you how appreciated and wanted you can be with another person. When you are cared for beyond the placated or patronized masses who will never know such joy, you will love being encouraged, worried over, longed for, and simply enjoyed for the rest of your life. To recall: Needing to feel important is not a dismissive, trivial affair for people. Love requires energy and work.

*Dale Carnegie – How to Win Friends and Influence People.

As these two very personal needs are closely related, we will touch on how to focus their momentum toward successes with romantic encounters above those you may already know. You will learn how to acquire a special knack for brighter friendships, memorable attentiveness in bed, and to celebrate the pivotal, outstanding ways in which you deal with everyday life.

> ### *The Single Most Important Gauge*
> ### *Of Everything We Are In Life…*
> ### *Is How We Treat The Ones We Love!*

IStockphoto

<u>*GREAT LETTERS OF PASSION !!!*</u>

William and Dionna have also brought us a highly spirited collection of Love Letters and Romantic Correspondence. They remind us that relationships expand with candid, loving inspiration. They grow with time, love, continued respect, and heartfelt physical interaction.

Even dynamic couples have to work to recalibrate their passion and intimacy. Stirring up regular exhilaration, great Lovers are credited with their continued willingness to try. Playfulness, mutual admiration, and a pleasing, sensuous lifestyle help magnify their ability to love each other for life.

Simply needing to be loved by someone is an understatement. We have to idolize each other and throw in some lovable pampering as well.

Intimacy between Lovers enhances physical attractiveness. No matter what shape our bodies are in, he might say, *"Oh, how beautiful she is to me in that light."*

She fawns over him, saying, *"He's so lovable and strong. He flexes so bravely for me. I just love him!"* Yet to sustain our emotional sincerity, we need to maintain an edict of mutual respect.

Reading or writing sensuous visions to one another is a wonderful place to inspire loving togetherness. Adding your own twist to how passionately you can flower your delivery will make your partner feel surprisingly beautiful and romantic again – in Love and in Life.

Great Letters of Passion are provided to spark your interactive creativity. Write letters of your own or feel free to use any of these to sprinkle your partner's name wherever there are references to "Darling', or 'Honey', or 'Baby', etc.

You control how often you send out a letter of Love. Remember, this is an extension of your care for each other, it's not meant to change you unwillingly. Print them out to read together and be enthralled! We all have passion waiting within us; take a moment to imagine the possibilities for you and your mate.

Below, you will find that **Great Letters of Passion** are daring elements for improving relationship enhancement. **'William'** titles are written from his perspective. **'Dionna'** titles are from hers.

Some letters are reflections of passionate conversation; friendly and loving in nature. Some tantalize the senses beyond the controllable realm. A few are graphically written, designed specifically to arouse and titillate you into your partner's loving arms. Go with your instincts for what works best then enjoy creating your own Letters of Passion and great romantic nights.

Letter Ratings Advisory: *Great Letters of Passion* are rated PG-13, R, and Adult. Some letters may not be suitable for certain readers.

Steamy, romance ahead, proceed with passion!

POEMAS de AMOR!
(POEMS OF LOVE!)
Written for you in Spanish and English.

Juan Francisco Ladero Guevara brings us a reflective collection of Romantic Poetry that will intrigue and inspire the latent, desirable companion in each of us. They remind us that even quiet relationships expand and grow when we add respect, imagination, and love to keep the embers ablaze.

Photo ©
B. T. Dormire

Ladero's poems focus on intrinsic events and experiences that affect a person or place in his life. Reading his work, we distinguish his visionary perspective and singular voice, appealing to the wishes of lasting intimacy. He breaks the shackles that continually bind us to loneliness.

And there *is* sorrow, separation, and loneliness within his poems. They are presented to help us overcome life with losses on our heart. Widowed or divorced, they allow us to envision a world with love renewed again in our lives.

Dynamic couples rejuvenate their fondness together. They remain stirred with each other when change is a part of their everyday being. This credits good Lovers with their willingness to always strengthen themselves and thrive.

Emotional intimacy between Lovers asks that we consider raising our intellectual connections as well. By reaching beyond ourselves and away from the comfort and relevance of everyday life, we transcend the benefits of simple, loving respect.

IStockphoto

We begin to admire a new graciousness inside the man or woman we thought we already knew.

Reading the harkened visions of this worldly Poet, or admiring any wistful artist at a city or national exhibit is a great place to inspire intimate togetherness. Adding your own twist to passionate, flowery compliments for your Lover will make them feel surprisingly romantic again.

Included within the pages of *Lasting Intimate Secrets*, you will find Mr. Ladero's poems a fresh and expressive path to dusting off your own relationship through the trials of life's experience. Some poems are the reflections of a passionate heart. Some tempt the senses into wondering how rueful love can actually get.

Is there a breaking point for the human heart? Can we crawl back from a point of no return? A few poems question where our truest desires belong. Do we lunge for our partner's loving arms, or stay in a comfortable, confident solitude instead?

Journey with **Juan Ladero** and enjoy reading his reflective collection of ***Poemas de Amor!***

~

Sharing Romantic Insights 1 – A Passionate Dreamy Place.

There's a place in my dreamy heart for you, my loving Woman. It's a great scene that has us running along a sunset beach laughing together or flying with galloping horses. We might even take a quiet walk instead. But we're holding hands as we go, dreaming of how to please each other even better than we did the night before.

When I suggest something extraordinary, you cling to my arm and ride along the journey for as far and as fun as it takes us. You find it lovely that I want you by my side so you hold onto me every step of the way. I find it lovely to feel you there as well.

I've walked with you through ocean froths and spread my toes with you in the velvet sand. We've trekked onto the tallest peaks and through the deepest valleys. I shared a headlamp with you on a night's walk down a long trail, protecting you from bears and flying saucers.

We grace each other in our lives and I fall more in love with you each day. It may be with the noontime sun beaming through your hair, or on nights under the dreamy stars. We are beautiful together as we move; we are even more beautiful together when we're finished. I adore the very thought of us entwined, never soaking up enough of our love, our kisses, or our hearts.

I love you for your looks – Oooh Baby, you're a looker! And I love you for yourself. You are a dream to me; smart, funny, an entire beauty unlike any other. And for you to love me the way you do in return, I am the luckiest man alive.

Thank you, Angel Face. Thank you, My Sweet.

IStockphoto

I. THE RECIPE FOR HUMAN EUPHORIA.

A. The History behind Sexual Improvement.

From the beginning of time, ancient cultures of the world have studied special techniques, disciplines, and motivations to perfect the art of sustaining great physical intimacy. The desire to maintain loving, mental endurance – or just plain competence – for both partners has been the subject of countless physiological and emotional studies.

Research by the sensual masters of the ancient Japanese, Chinese, and Indian civilizations have shown us through their cycles of movement *and* discipline that they were sustaining better intercourse for longer periods of time, and to rediscover that ability is the principal goal of this writing.

Love and devotion are equally important to our existence, and these tenants should not be overlooked just for the sake of our under-the-cover endurance.

Every culture through history professes that their distinct and particular methods of intimate contact are the most refreshing and desirable activities for dedicated couples. Transmitting pleasure through the varied range of physical and mental senses – through humor and touch and kindness – is inarguably the most descent human interaction we convey.

Expectations we have in our relationships are often based on contemporary biases. We see passionate lovers in our movies or the mystical ballet, or implications that a beautiful, heroic person is desired by another, and, we want to be like those people too.

We love what connects us to our favorite passion-borne icons, and why shouldn't we? We are constantly inundated by their media influences and physical attractiveness. We often emulate our Hollywood or Athletic idols in desire and form. But we want to stand out with our partners in real life. Either alone or in a crowd, we want to be as debonair or dashing to our mates as those 'other' likenesses are on the screen. We *need* to be loved with passion and honesty and we don't want anything less.

Harmony with a lover is for us the blossomed flower, the finished master-piece, and our thirst quenched from a hot desert jaunt. We learn that being in love, and loving to love in return can be very fulfilling. We become heroes to our partners in life, and them to us, and our hearts soar because of it.

Dionna's excerpt explains,

"My beautiful man, I long to make love to you in a tender, passionate setting. I want to hold onto you with every muscle I have for the benefit of our desire. I live not just for your physical contact and sexual release—any clown can do that without the thought of reason or romance in his heart to bring me to charms.

But I want your loving interest and compassion as well. I want to satiate your every pleasure, sharing myself with you immeasurably and with memorable effect, doing so to a state of exquisite frequency. I long for you completely and well within the laurels of my absolute content.

I will make love with you today if you wish, oh hero, and if you love me in return for the benefit of my own deep longing, then mine in that are all my dreams come true."

Dionna Jorgensen – <u>Nature of the Truest Lovers.</u>

While Eastern cultures may tout the liveliest physical lifestyles on earth, (et al, Kama Sutra from the deepest East; or Tantric Sex from India), why can't each of us in the West do the same? On further examination, many cultures resort to gadgets or numbing potions to quell overly excitable sexual reactions. On the other hand, 'toys' or devices, or prompts with pictorially sensuous images often serve to heighten the physiological response.

Men become quickly and overly aroused and have to work to physically control themselves from premature excitability.

As well, many women struggle to achieve a desired level of physical momentum that leads to an orgasm at all. Quite often, a woman has to *will* herself to the threshold of sustained and gratifying physical climaxes before her mate exhausts *his will* to bring her to that excitable state.

Riding the euphoria of amorous physical excitement and compassion over and over again is truly the bliss that charges all our sexual and emotional batteries. The delight we find in eager, participatory relations helps keep our mutual loves and desires alive.

IStockphoto

Poem 1. Amor Sumido. ~ Extinguished Love.

Poema de Amor #1

<u>AMOR SUMIDO</u>

Por qué te alejas,
de mi amor mío,
sí en tí pose,
mí amor escondido.

Supiste medrar en este
corazón impío,
cúal cabalgaba
antes memorable.

Por los arces
con faz de farándula
sin posar hacía,
tí, una mirada.

Pero ahora que pensaba
estar cerca de ti
siento que estas,
muy, pero muy lejos de mí.

Como lo estoy ahora
sobre la tierra
soñando por él
consuelo de tu amor.
Si de pensar,
en tu rostro,
en tu cuerpo,
de albor de niña.
Siento ser fácula
de oscuro amor inicuo.

Luego emprendo
mi largo viaje
en forma de flama
que ya se apaga.

Ladero

Love Poem #1

<u>EXTINGUISHED LOVE</u>

Why do you distant yourself
From me my love,
If in you dwells my hidden love.

You knew how to thrive
In this impious heart,
In which you rode so memorably.

Moving on,
Going about my dealings,
Without looking at you.

But now that I was intending to be with you,
I feel you are so far away from me.

Now I am standing on this earth,
Dreaming of your love's consolation.

Just thinking of your face,
Of your body,
Of the tree of a young girl,

I feel like a small torch
In a dark iniquitous love.

Next, I undertake my long journey
In the form of a flame
That is about to extinguish.

Ladero
Copyright ©1997 – 2015, Juan Francisco Ladero Guevara

B. Techniques to Improve Giving and Receiving Pleasure.

The Mental Half: Emotional intimacy for partners can be a chore sometimes when our bouts of physical contact are prolonged for more than a few weeks or months. A lack of mutual virility on command can be a nuisance that interrupts our fun as well. Euphoric rushes before either partner is ready, or the absence of sheer physical stamina to continue at will, might hamper an otherwise excellent naked and physical match.

The trouble with any well-intended romance is that we let our everyday lives get in the way of a clear path to attentive relations. The world of interruptions does nothing to encourage our loving, imaginative natures. The bills, the kids, the cars, the house, the job, the lack of money, too much money (*yes, this happens too*), the in-laws, junk in the yard, toys, the unfulfilled vacations, haughty business plans, one-sided exorbitant purchases, and so many other problems or unanswered dreams all pop into our heads when they shouldn't.

The only thing we both really desire is to be at peace with each other, to be alone and quiet with the one we love. Outside pressures though, constantly stymie our resourceful sexual abundance, not to mention our emotional stability and our confident sense of being.

So how can men and woman adjust their perspectives to isolate and include placing unencumbered sex and intimate physical comfort into their normal, bustling routines? How can we adorn a less stressful, more appreciative, and (ultimately) greater loving companionship with each other when all we think about is our everyday problems?

The answers to these and many other questions are coming up next. Follow along and see how easy you can move into the realm of extraordinary romance, and unequivocal love.

When you are with your Lover and you want to be as generous and physically giving as you've ever been – and it's just another end to a typical weekday – then frivolous interruptions have to be ignored. They need to be placed in a private corner of your mind for a while so you can be your absolute, total self with the person you love.

You can get exceptionally brilliant at intimacy by rethinking your approach to commitment and friendship with your mate.

Think about Time: After things have quieted down for the day, reserve a little time each night for getting close. For both of your own sanity checks, indulge in a special effort to help bring peace against your harried planet. Let nothing of the outside world intrude upon your companionship with a mate.

Force yourself to take a mental timeout for an hour or two. You're not ignoring the pressures of an impending financial or scheduling disaster in your life, you're simply standing back from them for a while. Specifically plan to deal with external issues later; you'll relax much more and be able to commit your mental and physical self to your mate.

Think about Money: Now we know this might be a stretch for some, but try to imagine that you have an endless supply of money in the bank, or at least not a lot of pending or devastating bills. This invariably helps us pretend that any financial pressures trying to overwhelm our more open natures with a great and willing lover, will not be given a chance.

Over time, throw some extra dollars into the vacation jar so you'll know that there is plenty of change in the coffer for a rainy day. Having the feeling of being financially free, acting *'As if you are totally secure in the world'* – even for only an hour – can have fantastic effects on your greater well-being *and* your physical and sexual appetite.

Think about Happiness: Plan an adventure together, *and then do it!* Arrange a getaway for a regular respite, or plan a beautiful vacation that is long overdue.

Cupid and Venus, The Louvre, Paris Photo by B.T. Dormire

Now, don't stress out making big plans for each other. Just get away from it all for a change. Leave the work, kids, and finances behind.

Go somewhere for yourselves!

Search out that Bed and Breakfast in a neighboring town, opt for a stay at your favorite mountain hideaway, or trek somewhere to the Peruvian Med'. But find something that will work for you both and follow through with it!

If only for a night, get a sitter for the kids; or trade 'child watch' with your family or a trusted friend – this doesn't cost a thing. Get together for a while with your partner and focus on each other again. The point is to plan a regular vacation event and not back down.

Peace can only come to you when you tame the interruptions. Learn to quell the endless worries and troubles of your life – at least for an hour or two. Fulfill your promise of renewed physical adventure with your 'significant other'. Rekindle love notes to each other in the morning before work. Appreciate the genuine friendship you have with your lover.

Find that special something missing in your usual routine. Bolster love back into your longing for mutual enjoyment. Know that the only one you care for is this great human being lying in your arms, and keep your desires at their peak to have some fun again. Don't worry if it has been a while since you've done those little things or think it's too late or silly to start anew. It isn't.

Be attentive to your Lover and your Romance will flourish.

Making Love in the Great Outdoors. Think about comfort and tranquility. What about the old Japanese and European walled or hedged in gardens? What about the private areas where creatures like the cats go to mate? They've got their seclusion figured out. We can too.

Romance in the forest or open country is still a highly untapped adventure in American life. The people of the cold and crowded spaces of Asia or Europe envy us for our generally good weather, wide open landscapes, and our vast, imaginative luxuries. If you can afford to leave your 'seriousness' at home once in a while, the great outdoors with its breezes, sounds, and delightful aromas totally awaits your attendance.

'We made love by a stream. When we finished, bells and birds
Sang us both to sleep.'

Be Loving in General! Kiss hungry kisses, make out long enough to get the juices flowing, hold hands, hug each other closely – this is what really thrives inside us. Always be respectful to him or her and remember not to overdo your Public Display of Affection (PDA). Unless you both really love it, this can go too far sometimes. Just know that loving, touching, and kissing your partner at every opportunity, makes for stronger, binding ties in your relationships.

Mental Training in a Nutshell–You have to be willing to block out the dreariest images that your thoughts invade upon your peace. Go rent and watch the movie – *What the Bleep Do We Know?* This film examines the very things we think about ourselves to MAKE US BETTER, or worse – it's up to us to find the difference and stick to it.

In a sense, the thrills attained in the back of the ole' Buick, or the suspense of getting caught out in the haystack on a glorious afternoon all play for a sensational experience. And besides, a little mischief or adventure can really revive your spirit.

But remember: **You have to take yourself there!** You have to be able to consciously transpose your emotions from fear and worry, to your personal 'Better Place' in thoughts and feelings. It's okay if you can't always adhere to these mental shifts, but romance and intimacy are a lot nicer if you can remember your abilities for tenderness and heartfelt love while you're with your lover.

~

You are my only...
Love comes with the dreams we have.
I strive to match them.

Btd.

If I Saw You!

Honey,

If I saw you in a busy street bazaar, or browsing through the trinket isles of a village market, I would be petrified to walk up and talk with you, but I'd do it! I would make every effort to win your attention and strike up a gallant conversation, hovering over the slightest word or two from your sweet lips. . . "Get Lost, Pal!"

That would send me howling with joy that you took a second of your time to brush me off. 'Wow, she noticed me enough to shoot me down! That's a start and I like it, I like it a lot!'

Spotting you on Rodeo Drive in some stylish boutique, I might find you sliding signature Weitzman's over your pretty feet. Without hesitation, I'd admire the angles of your legs highlighting their perfect fit. I would want to compliment your beauty on the spot.

Your prowess enthralls me as I watch you flex your legs in admiration. I'd watch you in wonder, astonished at how magnificent you really are to me.

But I HAVE seen you in these places, my Darling. I have watched you and held you closer than anyone ever has before. It isn't because people haven't loved you in your past; but more that I have the privilege to love you now.

Our times together are sweet. They hold a special air about them that only you and I have shared. It is fun for me, and it is right. Thank you for being my passionate, consummate Lover.

I hope your day is smooth, Baby. I hope it's cool, loving, and filled with at least one or two things you want to do for yourself.

Maybe you could order that velvety bedroom throe for us to take our spills and thrills – comfy, functional, and waterproof. Have it strewn across our King-size bed for a coconut oil surprise.

You could set up Yoga or Golf lessons for yourself on the sly. Ummm, surprise me when I get home. You may bend better than I do, but I know we would always play together well – golf, I mean.

But forever in your daily routine, you should relax for a moment and just think about us gently moving to a smooth, romantic song, closely holding our bodies to each other and wrapping ourselves lovingly in each other's arms.

'Either way, Good Morning, Honey. I'm thinking about our lives today.

I Love You,
Me

IStockphoto

W.J.

Your eyes thrill today Flowers bloom more radiant The Spring thaw has come.

Btd.

~

B. Techniques to Improve Giving and Receiving Pleasure. (con't)

The Physical Half: Sexual *expectations, inhibitions,* and *frustrations* versus *needs, desires,* and *love.* These all tie into juggling a great physical relationship with someone we adore. So how do we separate these two extremes without fouling up the ultimate intention of fun we want together? Can we keep this edict with us for good?

How can women feel attractive to themselves and constantly be refreshed inside their hearts? It's easy! By knowing how to motivate men into a state of constant emotional intimacy, they remain a Queen to anyone who has their radar is on for love. Can she move him with the silk of her touch? Yes. Can she keep his desire for a lasting physical connection no matter how far they are apart, no matter how simple, or sensual, or complicated their worlds are together? Again, yes!

All she has to remember is that she is absolutely beautiful to him when she smiles.

How can men who are decades out of their physical prime keep their emotional and romantic endurance going for as long as they want? How can some men profess to sustain their sexual techniques indefinitely? What if nature calls and a wild, energetic rush is imminent between them? Will he be able to hold back for his lover?

Can he keep his longing for her and treat her like the Queen she is in his eyes? Will he find time to stop for flowers and take-out on the way home after a tiring, million-hassle day?

Will he remember that she's the most important person in his life?

Every day, there are scores of opportunities to improve our sexual and emotional performance. But do we? Some examples may include: free-weight exercises, bike rides, trekking and hikes through a different beautiful valley every trip, regular physical health checkups, mental stimulation at an opera, ballet, or even a good Jimmy Buffet concert. Of course, physical intimacy would be great in itself. But quite often we treat these ideas as having nothing to do with good, strong, lasting, jubilant, sex.

Wow, well why not? Nothing could be further from the truth. Motivations like these perk up our stamina and recover our youthful approach to uninhibited love. They build upon relationship tools that are usually right in front of us every day. So how do we learn to recognize these 'together at last' moments and perpetuate them into our opportunities for love?

The path to these improvements are somewhat clearer than you may have thought. But consider that it's never as easy as a one stop shop, never as pretentious as the three word fix might seem after a catastrophic meltdown (*'I love you'*). You've got to do more than that. We want both of you to stimulate your imaginations and exist in abundant gratitude of each other for years to come.

When *Love* is in charge, it takes over, and you find yourself filling a hot tub with rose pedals from the flower section of your local market, or serving dinner with nothing on but an apron and a smile. You begin to do things for each other that reflects your everyday life. The new atmosphere in your world begs for great, unforgettable times as a mutually loving couple.

Building your Strength: Reserve a series of sessions each week for a good physical training regimen. There are many benefits to exercise if you strive to work out and get in shape. But you ask, "When do I have time to exercise?" Taking even a little time in your daily routine could substantially improve your appearance, outlook, and health.

People take pride in their bodies, their hygiene, and personal appearance. Loving partners tend to want to do the same in return. It's the mutual enjoyment of each other that stimulates confidence, productivity at home, and a boundless energy under the covers.

Set your clock a half an hour earlier in the morning and workout a little before you start your day – use Zumba or Yoga TV. Ask your boss for an extended lunch a couple of times a week to hit the gym – maybe agree to work the extra hour on those days to make up for being away from the desk.

When your day is drawing to a close, and while everyone else is rushing to get home, you go to your Sports Fitness Center and do your exercises at night after work.

It could answer your quest for the better, sexier lifestyle you've been hoping to find.

Building your Fitness: Gym memberships can cost a lot. They take up our time traveling to and from wherever they happen to be, and if we go out and buy extravagant fitness machines it can break the bank as well. So, consider these ideas……

A brisk walk or push-up, pull-up, leg squat, curl, or sit-up routine doesn't cost a penny!

For endurance, if you physically can't do any high-impact aerobics like a run, then a bicycle ride to the store and back is great for the legs. A swim can be luxurious! The nicest part about all of this is that it's absolutely free (except for maybe the pool, and the bicycle of course), and the rewards to your body are genuine.

Building your Happiness: Okay, since you've started to exercise, your outward physical appearance has improved and the attention you get from others boosts your inner confidence. They like what they see in your outlook and your newly improved physique. This rejuvenated step-up in overall physical health is a wonderful precursor to a sexier state of being.

When you exude a happier self-image, people tend to gravitate to that, wanting to be a part of the magic you've found. You interact more freely with others because of the attraction you have for their healthy looks as well. Your enthusiasm for such a new and positive life beams from every corner of your soul.

When you feel better about yourself and have more energy and bounce in your step, these likenesses will be extremely appealing to others – *especially, your Lover*.

Physical Training in a Nutshell – Take time to exercise to tone your muscles and endurance. Do this about 15 or 20 minutes each day if you can, or at least a couple times per week. Any active cardio-exercise helps to build your stamina as well as tighten up your abdominals, legs, back, and buttocks.

Ummm, Yummy!

Break your workout up into manageable parts. For the more advanced and ambitious of you, try to do a hundred push-ups, sit-ups, deep knee bends *(but not past the 90 degree angle)*, and at least that number for curls. Perform twenty of each exercise at a time, or whatever fits your physical abilities best.

Within as little as a week, your chest, shoulders, stomach, abs, and legs will take on new shape – *and strength!* (All of this is key to intimate prowess.) Your health will improve immensely and so will both of your loving, physical appetites.

~

Poem 2. <u>Rehacher Un Amor</u>. ~ <u>Remake A Love</u>.

Poema de Amor #2

REHACHER UN AMOR

Busco las noches estirpas del universo.
Busco el silencio en el viento.
Busco la amada lejos del tiempo,
sin que rehuya a mis sentimientos.

Yo no sé de palabras exageradas,
que se ahondan en el pensamiento,
que hacen latir y estragar los
sentimientos, para poseer a la mujer
amada.

Pero sí sé de aquellas
palabras, labradas en un lenguaje
tierno y sincero segregadas del corazón
y del alma,
ante la iluminación flamante
de su presencia.

IStockphoto

Ladero
Copyright ©1997 – 2014, Juan Francisco Ladero Guevara

17

Love Poem #2

<u>REMAKE A LOVE</u>

I look for the lost nights of the universe,
I look for the silence in the wind,
I look for my lover far away from time,

I don't know about exaggerated words
That penetrate deep in the thoughts,
Which pulsate and ravages emotions,
To possess the woman I love.

But I do know of those words,
Cultivated in a language that is tender and sincere
Separated from the heart and soul
Before the shining light of her presence.

Ladero
Copyright ©1997 – 2015, Juan Francisco Ladero Guevara

C. Intimate Desires and Discipline.

People long to improve their physical capacity, mutual intimate proficiency, and all the talents that encompass great, loving sex. Growth comes from increasing our strength, improving our inner outlook on life, or adjusting our attitudes to always think and say, "I love you Baby, now come over here and give me a big beautiful kiss!"

As we learn to care more ardently for each other, our love for giving the most wonderful pleasures to our mates come forth as well. But how can we keep our emotions and feelings in line with treating each other with gratitude and affection? Well, with just a little patience and effort, we're going to uncover the secrets to learn how to be a gallant lover again, right from the start.

What men can do for women: **Recognize Her Efforts** to be a good partner to you and *Do Something for Her!* Women are **motivated** by actions. They have daily grinds and sometimes they just want to rest.

Timing is everything when a man produces a simple, emotional gesture like cooking a wonderful meal, or giving her 'no reason' flowers, or placing an unexpected *'Thank you for You'* card on her pillow. Quite often this is the only spark she needs to send currents of heartfelt desire running through her veins. "He thought about me," she says. "He went out of his way to make me happy." Gentlemen, your rewards for these little efforts will be equally shared and unprecedented in her eyes.

Physical love should not be mandated as an entirely recreational activity; sometimes the other partner needs intimate conversation as well.

A beautiful romance is like an endearing symphony; they both have a special cadence of their own. You should make love to strengthen your bond together. But you gain points displaying a mutual appreciation for each other, seeking something magical that builds on your feelings of love and togetherness.

Know when the timing calls for uniting in different ways.

What women can do for men: **Recognize His Efforts** to be a good partner for you and *Do Something for Him!* Men are **stimulated** by actions. Showing him that you are eager and receptive for his touch gives you the power to make him feel more appreciated than he's felt all day. He can accept that there won't necessarily be any fireworks for the night, but quite often this is the seed that moves him to want to hold onto you until there are.

If it's been a week, a month, or longer between your bouts at physical love, then restore your emotional bond to each other with affection, compliments, absorbing talks by firelight, trusted disclosures, or talks about vulnerabilities and hopes. Take your time, your gratitude and passion for each other will rise gently between you again and then, your love will prosper.

Ideas for both of you. Add a nice candle to the atmosphere, or giftwrap a desert to your dinner-as-usual routine at the end of a typical day. Nothing fancy, just do a little extra something special to get him or her to smile. Send the kids next door for a few minutes because you want to cuddle with each other for a spell. Put on your favorite mood music, turn off the TV and sit with each other while listening to your favorite romantic CD. Quality time is what correlates to the physical – not just one partner dominating another when the timing is off.

Learning how to make wonderful, powerful love is an art in itself, and a topic beyond the scope of any one book. It takes strength as well as tenderness in just the right doses.

It takes an explorer's dedication with a will and a desire that is ready to examine any new potential for pleasing a mate.

It takes patience to turn the mundane into euphoria. Think a little harder, try a little more. In Spanish they would say, *"No hay mas pereza aqui"* – No more laziness here!

~

Passionate Letter 2. *Letters Apart.*
William & Dionna: Rated R

<u>Letters Apart</u>

Angel,

I want you to know that at this moment I am dreaming of us holding each other close. That as I think about going to sleep with you by my side, I know there won't be a stitch of clothes between us. I will nuzzle myself against your back to simply fall asleep lying next to you, holding you in my arms and smelling your sweet skin. I'm aroused by your moans, your softness, and how your back arches its way against me. I am stirred by your lips turning up to kiss mine while we lay together in bliss.

I love the way you love me, Baby, and I want to love you back as fully as you deserve. I want you to lay your body down, relaxed and ready, longing for my kisses on your every part, but not getting to them so quickly. Oh no, I want to tease you for a while, kiss the tops of your bare legs, massaging your thighs with the finest Eastern oils, and then looking across your full, lengthy body, seeing your hair in the soft candle light draped sensually over your shoulders, arms, and breasts. And with you by my side like this, I know there'll never be a reason for me to wish for anything else.

I love you, Angel. You are a fantastic part of my world and my life. I am the happiest man ever for finding you.

Forever Yours, My Darling.

W.J.

In Response to His Loving Note...

Dearest Lover,

Thank you, my sensuous, loving man. Indeed, it is hard to lie next to you, unclothed and not kiss and caress you in rhythmic motions, in response to our bodies moving together as one. I love it! I love you! Your kisses are so magical to me. They make me swoon in ways I never knew I could.

I want to press into you, Baby. I love to feel you hard against my back or between my thighs. It makes me excited to feel you. Sweetie, my legs want to open themselves up for you...right now!

I am sitting here, thinking about us together and all I see is you walking over and kneeling down in front of me as I sit in this chair, taking one leg and then the other, kissing them up and down...then passionately nudging me closer up to you. I want you to wrap your arms around my waist and kiss my bare belly as I wrap my legs around your back.

Reach up to my breasts and pay them good attention, kiss my ribs as they too deserve! Darling, taste my mouth in loving waves, like you did our first time out.

Then, my love, kiss me where you know you want to and where I am taken to a place that only you can bring me. Let me feel your sweet lips...let your fingers travel close to me, explore me, and tease me all the while. I am aching for your touch, longing for you to be with me, my oh-so sweet love.

Always Yours,
The Woman Who Knows
You like no Other!
D.J.

D.   An Intimate Journey toward Love.

When we transcend from emotional states to the physical – and back, what can lovers do to increase their ability to have shuddering, euphoric thrills **whenever** they want to – not because their physiology says they have to?

And what, if anything, can a woman do to physically prolong his efforts at pleasing her and thus, improve her climaxes as well?

The following ideas suggest that no matter how strong or insecure we may feel under the covers, there is hope for the untrained lover. We are going to outline a few simple ideas you can apply to your everyday life to enhance your future of promising, sexual events.

Despite our often frustrating abilities to have an orgasm *when we decide we're ready*, people do have a pretty good time at sex. By all means, it shouldn't be any other way. But it isn't enough is it? We want more romance, want it in soothing and luxurious places, and we want the feeling to last for as long as we can stand it.

• **SECRETS for MEN:** Many men are often burdened both physically and mentally with the problem of having an untimely ejaculation once a blissful interlude has begun with a woman. Men are apologetic, women are sympathetic and intimacy becomes less and less frequent and more like an overplayed, tiresome chore; not like the gift or even spiritually uplifting experience it is meant to be.

Satisfaction for both lovers goes unquenched because of a shortened physical experience for him and thus, no orgasm reached for her during intercourse. He is dissatisfied because he neglected to bring her to climax. She is dissatisfied because she couldn't succumb to the gallant efforts made by her promising man. As trite and feverish as his extracurricular sensations may have been, he simply couldn't 'do it' with her long enough to meet her needs.

As premature ejaculation inhibits a couple's overall pleasures for sexual fulfillment, the necessity to enlighten people about the physical and mental alternatives to this is being more freely discussed.

Other debilitating factors arise from an infrequency of sex between partners. The more routine and complacent people get with each other, the less sexual activity there seems to be between them.

~

William & Dionna Jorgensen

Briefly speaking about relationship apathy, have the two of you gotten so bored or dismal with each other in bed that nothing works anymore? Why aren't you making progress in your commitment to each other? Do you feel violated when you have sex with your partner? Do you feel like the violator instead? While YOU may encourage passion and romance to save the relationship, are these ideas landing on deaf ears? Does it seem childish to your partner that you have these desires all the time? Maybe it's time for relationship counseling or professional arbitration for the two of you to get back on course.

Do you feel loved by your mate?
Does your mate feel loved by you?
Have you asked?

Some people don't care if their partners are thrilled or not. This goes for the men who satisfy themselves with one quick romp and then roll over and go to sleep, or the women who refuse sexual intimacy with a healthy, caring partner for months and months. They are all missing out on the entire saga of human, physical enjoyment at its very best. We'll just have to pity the more fruitful partners in this unsteady match and hope they find an easy solution to their dilemma.

People are looking for answers. They are tired of hearing about what is possible and what is not, or what it takes to get things right with their mate – like everyone else is entitled to some sort of impenetrable secret, but not them.

The most rewarded people are those who want the best for themselves *and* their mates, no matter how much effort it takes. There are many of us who long to improve, many who feel a need to become strong for our lovers; mentally, physically, and spiritually. We are the ones most willing to chase that 'Intimate Journey to Paradise'. We are the ones who desire those long sought-after, *Lasting Intimate Secrets* being held so guarded and so dear.

Sometimes, the quality of sexual relations may be enhanced by abstaining for as much as a week or more, maybe even a month. But to neglect each other's attention for too long only increases the desire levels beyond that of having sex for a pleasing, fulfilling duration. In other words, if he's too excited, he's going to explode too soon. The cycle of frustration begins anew.

24

Poem 3. Filoso Fando El Amor. ~ Meditating About Love.

Poema de Amor #3

FILOSO FANDO EL AMOR

En una de mis tardes.
estábame preguntando:

¿ El amor tiene algun deslino?
¿ Se basa en una Fiel eternidad?

Pero gente toda diganme:¿
Amor en todas partes existe?

Comparábame con una mariposa
cual capa de mil colores vestía
si como ella. Yo había de infringer
en el pacto de cuanto amor exista.

Luego decíame infundado:
¿ de amor necesidad tengo yo?
Finalmente decía.

Me basta yá esta vida, sin Amor.
Que sin mas sabe a problemas y desdicha.
Que un amor entero tiempo requiera.
En sum undo de alegría y Fantasía,
Pero para Usted....

Ladero

William & Dionna Jorgensen

Love Poem #3

MEDITATING ABOUT LOVE

One afternoon I asked myself:

Does love have an end?
Is it eternally faithful?

Tell me, people:
Does love exist everywhere?

I compared myself to a butterfly
That wears a coat of a thousand colors
I was about to infringe the covenant of any love that exists.

Later I unfoundedly told myself:
I need love?
I finally said it.

I've had enough of this life without Love.
There are only problems and unhappiness.
More than love alone can handle.
In short, I dismiss joy and fantasy,
But for you.....

Ladero
Copyright ©1997 – 2015, Juan Francisco Ladero Guevara

26

Secret #1 for Him: Character, Charisma, Charm, Chivalry, Consideration!

Nothing is more impressive to a Woman

Than a focused, attentive Man.

The ability to combine the above edicts into one general theme holds true to the fabric of an unending, undivided love for someone. The funny thing about these traits is that if you live a dignified, honorable life, you shouldn't have to seek them at all – they are already within you. But to lead you to even more intimacy together, with lives that are filled with growing passions, love, and understanding between you and your mate, we'll list a few here to spark your memory:

You can name a hundred different things that would impress your Sweetheart, but for starters how about...

Honesty, honor, integrity, trustworthiness, faithfulness, love, friendship, kindness, attention, a good sense of timing, quality attentiveness, commitment, opening her doors, holding her hands, kissing like it might be your last, kissing so she'll remember it for hours, days, or even weeks from now. Accepting her the way she is, believe in her dreams, listen to her and interact with eagerness and passion. Being loyal, being dedicated, encourage her when she wants something more, show compassion, have unending tenderness, maintain strength, keep impeccable hygiene, stay healthy, have flawless character, appreciate her. Keep admiration for her with enjoyment, peace, and sound loving principals in your heart. Maintain respect, creativity, and longing for her, love every physical inch, never let her body hit the sheets without your hands behind her. Use guidance, thoughtfulness, forgiveness, wonder, and laughter. Be her rescuer, be her driver, be her prize fighter, be her lover and friend, be her confidant, defend her, enlighten her, astonish her, surprise her, help her, please her, and finally, above everything else – never stop believing that she totally deserves a great life with you in it.

She'll always love you for it. You'll always want to improve physically and mentally to keep great passion between you. You'll want to do more for her than you've already done. It's a loving circle that melts in to itself and has no end.

Chivalry – here's a rarely mentioned item, but consider that a **woman** needs to feel emotionally connected to want to make love to a man. And in the very same notion, a **man** needs to make love to feel emotionally connected to a woman. It's almost a Catch-22! Chivalry asks **both of you** to remember this and try to recognize these traits in each other. If you keep your emotional electricity at a peak and your devotions sincere then she'll feel loved and he'll get what's coming to him. *(Principally, some ooh-la-la and not a night in the doghouse).*

So, speaking of love, we'll now move into the more physical terms that enhance the efforts and considerations you instill from the added suggestions above.

But First…

~

Passionate Letter 3. *Hello My Lover.*
Dionna: Rated Adult

Hello My Lover

Hello My Lover,

You never cease to amaze me. I believe that just your words alone could sustain me. Your letters are so beautiful. Your openness is unique and rare…I love you so much for this. I love that you can describe with such fluid detail the actions of our love and passion. As you describe to me where you are kissing me, touching me, and loving me…my body shivers in remembrance and excitement and I feel you next to me, on me,…in me…though we are thousands of miles apart.

We are beautiful together, my sweet Baby. Thank you for taking that first chance with me. You spent time and effort to engage me into your life and love. How lucky I am to have you.

We have lived well for years now and I feel there is so much more to experience. We have so much more growth to achieve. I am thrilled by the thought of us together at night.

Sweetheart, I am sitting here writing you and my body is throbbing, thinking about us as one. My skin is full of excitement for us. I envision you behind me moving your hands underneath my blouse, kissing the golden hairs on the small of my back. Your hot, tender breath is elevating me to passion.

Then your hands find my breasts, freed from their daily binds, cupping them in your hands, massaging me softly, moving your fingers firmly across them as you kiss my shoulders with your sweet lips and hot mouth.

By now I have pushed my back into you and I reach around to feel you through your silk pajamas. As we grasp each other, you wrap one strong arm around my body, continuing to love me with every kiss, and your other hand moves toward my tummy, teasing me...Oh, how I love that... You feel my excitement. I want your love...all of your love...with me and in me. I turn and slide down your chest as I am greeted by your full, exciting love. I sweetly kiss you all over, taking you into my mouth, enjoying you. I want to make out with you, Baby, feeling you rise and share your love with me...yet I also want you as one with me so badly now...let me have you...love me!

I know we are going to kiss passionately from my mouth down all of my body to the tops of my feet. I also know you will not neglect to kiss and make love to that special place that knows only your lips, your amazing love. It thrills me so. I love to feel you kiss me there right on my most exciting part.

and then feeling you swirl around me and slide next to me, it is SO exciting…just the thought of it, makes me want to explore you too and shudder together, right now…ooooooooh, mmmmmmh. Yes Baby.

You bring me to such ecstasy…your fingers…I can't think of anything else….you have me…there is nothing I can do, but let go and let the rush and euphoric feelings envelope and take me…I love you inside of me, it feels so perfect…My excitement is rising and you are one with me, making it last and taking me over another wave of passion and love…you continue to shower me with your love. Could I be more satisfied? No, I think not…at least not until we start to love again!

I Adore You, My Sweet Man,

D.J.

Dionna

~

Secret #2 for Him: Control and Mechanics!

Over controlling your sensitivity may hinder you from prolonging the sexual act no matter what kind of trick you employ with a prop. Maybe the answer is to seek the counseled advice of a physician who specializes in performance enhancing measures to either activate or temporarily numb the sensory nerves around the rib of the penis.

There are many sources of sexual numbing creams, many available to you without a prescription. Some good creams are found on mature Internet sites, others are right there in the adult stores and novelty shop outlets that can enhance erection stamina. The Kama Sutra product line has some good ointments, as do many other brands.

Emla Cream, prescribed under a physician's care, is made up of among other things, 2.5% Lidocaine, and 2.5% Prilocaine, and is very good at attaining these sexual goals.

Allow it to work for 45 minutes or so before making love and it will desensitize the penal nerves enough for an hour or more of continued physical interaction.

YOU MUST CLEAN OFF the cream prior to penetration with your mate (basically for the reasons described in the Warning below) and remember, the goal of increasing your endurance is to ultimately do so without the help of creams or tricks to enhance your performance. **(Warning: adverse reactions to this or any Topical Drug may result in serious physical complications or unrecoverable health risks, talk to your Doctor before using any medical treatment.)**

Men, once you understand the reactions your body undergoes and how to recognize the pulsing, climactic signals shooting from your brain to your stimulated nerves, you will be able to hold and sustain the euphoria at will. She will shudder and thrill at your every delicate touch, and you will be able to hold on to your own excitement as she enjoys these sessions more and more. She might even resort to yelling out your name in the rush of these loving extremes.

Mechanics! Quoted from the sexual health information site – www.goaskalice.Columbia.edu:

"**The ancient Chinese** used a small O-ring device to help deter and subsequently intensify the male ejaculation process. Historically, they were quite specific in nature and made of ceramic, ivory, or jade. It was placed at the base of an erected penis – not at the rib near the top of his shaft. Today, many are made of soft leather or other flexible plastic or rubber material. Usually, they have a snap or pressure knob for quick release right at the time of orgasm.

"Avoid using O-ring substitutes: rubber bands, binder clips, and vices, for example, for these cause too much constriction. The ideal ring stays in place when the penis is soft, yet it can smoothly slip off or unsnap when it gets hard. Lube can be added to make putting rings on and taking them off a little easier. Contemporary examples can be found at www.adamandeve.com.

"For safety and pleasure, an O-ring needs to increase the size of the erection only slightly.

If you notice more pronounced swelling, then the fit is too tight. In that case, take the O-ring off immediately. **It's also vital for men to take off their O-ring at the first sign of pain or if the genitals feel cold.** In addition, it's dangerous to leave a ring on for too long, as well, DO NOT wear one to sleep when spontaneous erections are all the rage.

"**Caution:** An erection of several hours can cause blood coagulation in the penis, making it difficult to lose the erection. This is called Priapism, a prolonged erection. Since new blood cannot enter the penis, this can be severely painful and cause permanent damage to the erectile tissue. If this happens to you, seek medical attention as soon as possible, and don't worry — the staff at the ER has seen this (condition) before." *Alice*

Some O-rings come affixed with a small knob at the apex of the ring to act as a stimulus for the clitoris, it serves mainly to restrict the blood from retreating from a healthy erection before, during, or after a relishing orgasm. It should not be too tight because the male physiology still has to operate. And unless there is a definite tension release on a more flexible, contemporary O-ring, the semen will ejaculate backwards into the bladder. Not a real problem, but this can become discomforting over time.

In today's world, a good, operable O-ring can be found through your Google or Yahoo search engines with the keyword 'Cockring'. And again, you can find them in adult book stores and novelty shops that sell sex toys. It can help alleviate any *Short Fuse* problems you may have while making love and building your endurance.

Erectile Dysfunction! (ED)

Eeee-gads! What the heck is this?

As age and anxiety begin to affect our performance in bed, there are times when it seems that we just can't perform to our peak as much as we'd like. Erectile dysfunction affects about 30,000,000 men in the U.S. and age is not always the determinant. Diet, weight and physical condition, and even anxiety can take its toll. But there *are* several prescribed blood flow accelerators to help with this debilitating affliction.

The most popular inflow enhancer medications are VIAGRA, CIALIS, and LEVITRA.

There are others, but these medicines should be prescribed by your doctor and they can help a man, in most cases, with ED get and keep an erection when he is sexually stimulated. It is rare to reach an erection just by taking these medicines.

ED is usually caused by something physical, such as a disease, injury, or side effects from other drugs. Diseases most commonly associated with ED are high blood pressure, cholesterol, diabetes, and some cancers. Lifestyle and psychological factors can also play a role in causing ED, such as smoking, drinking, and stress.

Here are a few suggestions to help avoid negative lifestyle factors that can cause ED:

- Find ways to stay more active (mow the lawn, walk the dog, learn to dance, join a gym).

- Help manage your weight by eating healthy and watching your portion size with meats and starch.

- Reduce consumption of colas – diet or otherwise.

- Drink less alcohol. Do less cannabis.

- Commit to end smoking for life. The positive results are significant.

- Look for ways to reduce stress in your daily routine. Visit www.AnthonyRobbins.com for great lifestyle suggestions and guidance in this ever-budding realm.

Only your doctor can determine if VIAGRA (sildenafil citrate) or other enhancers are right for you. VIAGRA isn't for everyone and precautions to differing drug interactions should not be ignored. Go to www.WEBMD.com and search for Erectile Dysfunction for a more thorough discussion.

Taking these enhancers help to achieve two things for men in their intimate relations. First, and most obvious, is enabling him to attain a full and wholesome erection. Second, is to last a greater period of time so she can reach the orgasmic plateau and take in wave after wave of euphoric bliss.

Men, the end game of everything discussed above, is a workable desensitization of the male arousal response and a lasting pleasure for both you and your partner.

Working to control your physical excitement can eventually free you of devices or prescribed enhancements to help you master the art of unassisted, freewheeling intercourse.

The ultimate goal here is to wean you away from premature release and get you into a more relaxed, controlled level of interaction. Learn to hold back the explosive responses on your own and continue to satisfy each other without the help of a tool.

You determine when the time is right for your loving, shuddering thrills.

~

Poem 4. <u>Mitsy</u>.

Poema de Amor #4

<u>MITSY</u>

*Sí, cansada por la tarde
de oscuro semblante,
navega la tortuga Mitsy
de largo pataleo
suren en ramajes el agun
del verda paraniso.*

*Su cúpuln durn como la espada
suave y semsible de alma navega,
tal vez como una más
del olenje, nacé y muere
a cada sumergida.*

*Canaadabya por la tarde
alterna con la noche.*

Ladero
Copyright ©1997 – 2015, Juan Francisco Ladero Guevara

Love Poem #4

<u>MITSY</u>

Yes, she is tired because of the dark feature of the afternoon,
Mitsy the tortoise navigates.
From long flutter kicks, arise the branches of the green
paradise.

Her shell is hard like a shield,
With a gentle and sensitive soul navigating inside,
Perhaps like another one of the waves,
It comes to life and dies each time it submerges.

Bordering the afternoon,
Exchanging with the night

Ladero
Copyright ©1997 – 2015, Juan Francisco Ladero Guevara

Secret #3 for Him: Discipline!

The Skills to "Start and Stop". This encompasses an approach to making love that improves sexual endurance by starting and stopping your intercourse and giving her steady moves in and out before you flood your love all over her stomach and chest. Not a bad idea in and of itself, but you want that to happen at your command, not some frantic, last minute improvisation.

Again, *Alice* recommends that you rethink what lasting longer means – that it has to do with teaching your body a new way to respond. You can learn to slow down, to recognize the "point of no return" (the moment right before your orgasm is inevitable), to back away as you get closer to the ultimate rush, and to postpone the inevitable to a more desirable time.

When you work up to the point of a climax, STOP!

As you begin to physically surge together, discontinue any overly-sensitive movement whatsoever. Neither you nor she can react to even the smallest vaginal quiver or you will lose it with her for sure. Back away for a moment and let the desire subside. Now, once you've held on, move up and down her body, kissing her in places you know will send her to the moon. But don't go back inside of her again until you can hold back the climactic, primordial urge.

The "Start and Stop" technique improves your sexual virility. It takes discipline and control and a little practice, but it can take you to the limits of human pleasure and keep you there without the accessories mentioned in *Secrets 2* above. Go ahead and work together on this. Move your naked bodies as one, slowly working alongside and in and out of each other, traveling into each other a little farther and a little gentler with each successive lunge.

When you feel the rushing and rising of tensions starting to build again, then stop, back out from her (gingerly though – so as not to erupt on her unannounced) and then wait, or more suitably, move on down for some oral stimulus to keep her engines at peak.

You may even go as far as saying aloud or to yourself, "Stop!" and this cue allows you both to let the power and throbbing fade to more manageable levels.

It certainly helps you control more of your body's reactions by learning to recognize the pressures that build up before you climax. The object is to condition yourself not only with good physical strength, but with each and every intimate session to be able to keep going with her for longer and longer periods of time, releasing *when you want to* and not a moment before.

~

Passionate Letter 4. *I Miss You Very Much.*
Dionna: Rated Adult

I Miss You Very Much

Hello Handsome

How was your night, Sweetheart? I hope it was beautiful.

I miss you very, very much...so much so that I'll go to bed naked and think of you and me together...skin to skin...I will want to move up next to you and swagger my hips into you giving you the hint that I am feeling sexy and turned on. I will want to feel your warm bare skin next to mine. I want you to touch my body and feel my curves and know instantly that I long for your love. I want to imagine your talented hands running over my hips and legs and in that special place that I am wet and excited, wanting you, my man. I will reach over and feel you, firm and excited to my touch as well. I want you.....and will have you as mine this new day to come!

Good morning, my Love.
D.J.

38

In Response to Her Loving Note...

William writes:

Good Morning to you my Angel,

I always anticipate our reunions together, and in between those times, we grow and move closer together through our letters and phone calls, and we make love with each other over the miles. I love imagining our bodies sliding over and around each other's skin from head to toe, responding to my kisses and fingertip caresses and touches from my lips.

I often think of us in wonderful places, hugging and cuddling so silky smooth with each other and loving you peering over banisters or out the open windows of our private villa, or Parisian balcony. I imagine your legs sliding up alongside mine, and how their velvety touch thrills me to passion. I feel your hands against my chest and your hips pressing into mine as well. You brush your breasts across me and I take them with my kisses and feel these sensations all the

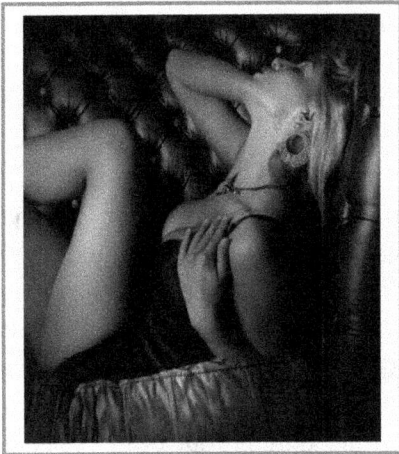

way to my toes. My legs wrap around your lower back and I hold you closer to me and we're more fully engulfed than we've ever been before.

Our intimacy rises with each exciting breath. Our privacy submerses in our world, as only true lovers can know.

I long for you to kiss me, and I long to kiss you in return.

You are a beautiful lover to me and I want you more than you can know.

Your Best Man Ever!
W.J.

~

Secret #4 for Him: Talents!

Combining Intimate Kisses and Hands! Men, if you have never considered the passion of giving her a great session of oral sex, then you need to reconsider it for both your sake. You need to learn about a woman's anatomy and precisely where the clitoris is set. Some women have a very pronounced, elongated condition, and others have a more recessed, harder to locate protuberance. Google the keywords 'Finding the G-Spot' and learn from these references.

But as each woman is different in this regard, so should a man's techniques be mixed to arouse her to climax. Unfortunately, some men believe that 1, there's only one way to perform oral sex, applying the same method for every situation 'down there', or 2, there's a mysterious barrier below her navel that shouldn't be trespassed. They halt their advance because of a woman's natural scent, or that they're afraid of the taste.

Gentlemen, understand that when a woman has cared for herself, cleaned herself up and is healthy and thriving, there is nothing that smells sweeter and nothing that tastes greater. You have to get past the bees to get to the honey, but when you do, it's the icing on the cake! When she gets wet and hot, she is waiting for you to make love to her fully and completely, and going down on her is just part of the wonderful soufflé' experienced with sex and life. *(Besides fellas, if you don't do it, you're in a bunch of hot water).*

The Third Base Hit! If you find that you just can't sustain your passionate intercourse without an explosion of the dreamiest kind, then intersperse your penetrations with your most skillful oral and fingering-sex techniques. Combining kisses and gentle swirls of your tongue while including the gentle thrust of your fingers into her sweet warm mound will have her climbing the bed rails to her many sustainable peaks.

Adding two-fingers to the inside of her during your oral escapade, simulating your usual erection in width and depth, and simultaneously touching just the right spots with your moist, giving mouth, you will have her calling out your name before it's over, wondering who you are and what planet you're from.

You need to know the right speeds and pressures she requires — conditions that constantly change depending on the woman, her mood, and your patience — before, during, and after all her breathtaking orgasms.

Study Hard!

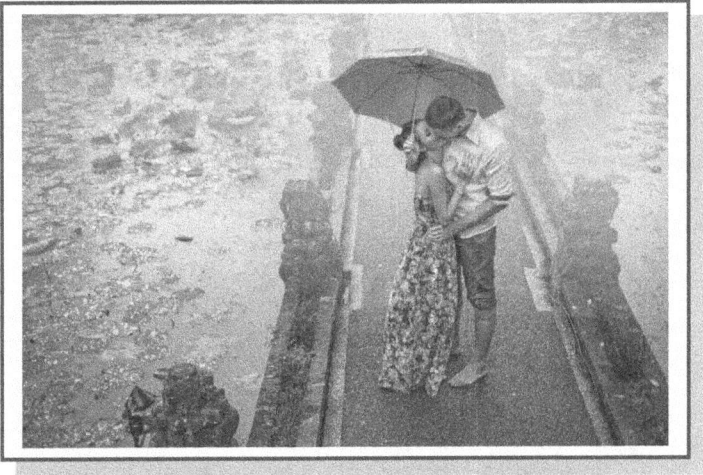

~

Poem 5. La Morada Del Viento ~ The Wind's Abode.

Poema de Amor #5

LA MORADA DEL VIENTO

Vuelve Norma Jean a la ancha avenida
morada del viento.
Allí te espero y te esperaré siempre.
Coge tus libros, tu bandera, tu ideal,
toma la tierra, planta un árbol,
agita tu bandera, y arroja la simiente:
abriré el surco con el buey arabor/
¡ El orbe es tuyo, mio, de vosotros.

Mi morada es de idilios,
también de combate.
Mi fusil va a la diestre, las zarpas
acechan a lo lejos.
¡ Yo soy el viento, centinela del orbe!
Mi canto es de guerra, de amor o de paz;
vuelve Norma Jean a la ancha avenida,
ya llegó la alborada, hoy mi canto es de amor,
de siembra y de esperanza.
¡ Yo soy el viento, centinela de tu amor,
fiero en la batalla!

Y me preguntas Norma Jean por mi morada:
Yo soy de la tierra del indómito puma,
del majestuoso condor y taciturno buho
hijo del Ande, viento, hermano del cactu,
donde el sol no de pones, ni la luna mengua,
del rincón de muertos de libérrimos hombres,

¡ *Donde un puñado de tierra,*
es una tumba pocra!
Ven a mi morada Norma, tú amor me hace falta,
ya tengo la tierra, el buey y un canto de amor!
Echa la simiente, pacer mis rebaños,
arma tu choza y arrulla un niño;
¡Ha vuelto la aurora, es tiempo de amar!

Mañana, quién sabe
No estaré para la cosecha,
No te olvides de me Norma Jean.
Te amé en el fragor de la batalla
al borde de los surcos,
en la siembra o en la cosecha,
a la sombra de los sauces melancólicos.
Allí te esperaré siempre, siempre.

Mañana quién sade,
habré caido en la refriega,
no te olvides de mi Norma Jean.
Si es hora de partir, solo debo pebirte,
para mi tumba un puñado de tierra,
de tierra pocra del "rincón de muertos"
de libérrimos hombres;
y un himno de paz,
y ¡ Paz infinita en el orbe!

Ladero

Love Poem #5

<u>THE WIND'S ABODE</u>

Come back, Norma Jean, to the wide avenue,
To the wind's abode.
I await you there and I will await for you always.
Take your books, your flag, your ideal,
Take the earth, plant a tree,
Wave your flag, and broadcast the seed:
I will open the furrow with the plow ox.
The earth is yours, mine, ours.

My abode is made of idylls,
And also of strife.
My rifle is on the right, the talons
Lurk afar.
I am the wind, the sentinel of the world!
Mine is a song of war, of love or of peace;
Come back, Norma Jean, to the wide avenue,
The dawn has arrived, and today mine is a song of love,
Of sowing and of hope.
I am the wind, the sentinel of your love,
Fierce in battle!

And you ask me, Norma Jean, about my abode:
I am from the land of the untamed mountain lion,
Of the majestic condor and the taciturn owl
A son of the Andes, the wind, brother of the cactus,
Where the sun does not set, nor the moon wane,
From the corner of the completely free dead men,
Where a handful of earth,

Is a pocra* tomb!
Come to my abode, Norma, I need your love,
I have the earth, the ox and a song of love!
Broadcast the seed, pasture my flocks,
Make your hut, and lull a child to sleep;
The dawn has returned,
It is time to love!

Tomorrow, who knows
I will not be here for the harvest,
Do not forget me, Norma Jean. I
loved you in the clash of battle
At the border of the furrows,
During the sowing or during the harvest,
Under the shade of the melancholic willows.
I will wait for you there always, always.

Tomorrow who knows,
I will have fallen in the skirmish,
Do not forget me, Norma Jean.
If it is time to part, I must only ask you,
For my tomb a handful of earth,
Of pocra earth from the "corner of the dead"
Of completely free men;
And a hymn of peace,
And infinite peace in the world!

*Place where the City of Huamanga, Peru was founded.

Ladero

Copyright ©1997 – 2015, Juan Francisco Ladero Guevara

"Will you love me today, Baby?"

IStockphoto

"Yes, Angel. I think I will."

Secret #5 for Him: The Kiss and Desirable Affections!

The Kiss. Saved for the very last, the 'Kiss' is no secret, but good ones are the single most important prelude to any loving adventure between couples in love. If there are any barriers to a relationship, discomforts that impose a hindrance to advanced experiences in bed, it probably stems from someone who doesn't accurately or passionately know how to kiss.

Kissing: Practice Makes Perfect. How do you describe a good kiss? Should we kiss with passion every time? It helps, but isn't always necessary if we apply a few simple techniques to make each kiss a pleasing effort. From a peck on the cheek to a full-fledged mouth to mouth embrace, kisses range from soft to firm, but in most cases they should definitely be with excitable, memorable affection.

Kisses should have some tension in the lips so as not to clack the teeth together. But they should also be soft enough to feel the sensual connection that ensues between your lips. Short of the basic arousals of a passionate kiss, being sensual is what makes someone want to find out what's next.

Why the Kiss. Working from the standpoint of simply an evening of love, we'll cover the anatomy of kissing and the idea of how to arouse a partner from the beginning of your passionate throws to collapsing in sexual exhaustion and sleep. Clean, sweet, fresh breath goes a long way too. So get ready to inspire, be inspired, and enjoy the suggestions that follow.

William: Kissing to me is like playing the Piano. Little notes begin the symphony. I like starting in any of the upper erogenous regions. Kissing the top of her hand, slowly and methodically, turning her arm over and kissing her lightly from underneath her wrist to the top of her elbow is a good way to start. Next, I'll work my way up along her biceps inside and out, then to her shoulders, maybe the back of her neck with little suckles to get things in motion. I kiss her like I'm catching the juice from an apple or peach dripping down the side of each cheek.

I will embrace her to arousal with hints of my teeth and tiny suckles. It starts the tingling from there.

Dionna: I love it when he reaches my shoulders. He'll nibble a bit and remind me of his sharp, strengthened bites. And when I turn my head away with imaginative passion, he works around my collar bones and neck until I come back around to his mouth in love and begin to kiss him in return. He has championed himself at kissing me in just the right doses. He'll move down one side and up the other, never neglecting an inch of my skin, reading my thoughts with where I'd like to have him next. He'll tease me by going down to my pelvis then he'll curl back up around my side and find my ribs with his face and teeth, gently rubbing and toying around my stomach with his lips. Sweetly, he's probing my reactions until it's time to kiss my legs.

William: I love her legs, long and beautiful. They are her most powerful elements that wrap around my thighs and bring me closer to her body, never letting go, always relaxed enough for me to hold one in my arms to kiss and surprise her with my lips. As my hands caress her from underneath a calf or one of her knees, I move my kissing, suckling teases across the vast expanse from one thigh to another. Back and forth I go, slowly and deliberately working closer to her treasured prize. And when I'm finally there, parting her with my mouth as she has waited, ready and patient, my kisses take on a whole new element of arousal. It's as if we were starting all over again, from the gentle touch of my moistened lips, to fully making out with her there with all the passion we can stand.

Dionna: I pulse and throb inside my body. It's as if a great locomotive is starting on a long journey and I love to heave my breasts and entire being into getting over the mountain. He has brought me to euphoria again and I climb along with him to our rendezvous with an impassioned union. Together we are lying naked and peaked, sliding into and over each other with our loving, hungry kisses. In his obvious excitement I am relaxed and open, waiting to envelop him, waiting to receive his everlasting pulse.

~

Before she explodes: Just before she peaks – apply tender, teasing, kisses on and around her clitoris, working over her entire body, up and down, and side to side. Together with little tongue caresses, a gentle sucking here and there, and mild, steady pressure will have you both hot and ready for climax. Then add your fingers and massage her G-Zone.

It's certainly the kind of arousal that thrusts her into an ultimate climb to orgasm and thus pressing her whole body against you. But realize that when you finally get the right combination of pressure and cadence her moans will increase. When you are finally on the stimulated target, this doesn't necessarily mean to increase the pressure or get more excited thinking you're doing her a favor. She'll let you know if she wants more kisses and how to apply them.

During her orgasm: Now begins the rush. As she starts to erupt and her body reacts, her breathing is going to heighten and her undulations are going to increase. An exciting conclusion to giving her a clitoral orgasm, with the work of your mouth and hands, is to finish the event by climbing up her body to kiss her lips with yours and give her the fullest intercourse you can muster.

Be gentle with the initial thrust, but move into her slow and deep, gaining speed as she demands it with her body. Before she succumbs to the orgasmic rush, she may very likely have a simultaneous vaginal orgasm, which in terms of the electricity between your two bodies, will have you both climaxing together in harmonious bliss.

It is important to develop a talent of when to continue your gentle, physical applications or when to back off and subside. Men need to do this to help sustain the thunder for her, or, when needed, to return to gentle, slow caresses of her body – if, to touch it at all. Tenderly bring her entire, throbbing body back to planet earth until she's ready to stop for the night, or start up again for some more.

After her orgasm: Once again, too much pressure and she'll have to back off, too little and she won't reach another peak. Men can surely relate to this for the sensitivity we have in our own response.

We're quite tender to the touch just after orgasm, and to completely regenerate for another session usually takes us about 15 to 20 minutes. With women, it's more like 3 to 5 minutes, much quicker to roll into the next climactic plateau. Some women can last wave after wave, so guys, you better be ready!

Applying the right amount of post-climax attention is the key. Not too much, and not too little. If she's still lubed up and eager, you will have her right back into an orgasmic fireworks array. If you are patient and caring, you'll know through her responses if you've mastered the touch.

Beware though! In getting better at these techniques, she may begin to ask you to love her in the most precarious places. She may plan a little session for you atop the Eiffel Tower overlooking a romantic, nighttime Paris. You may get jumped on the kitchen counter near the cookie jar after your morning egg soufflés. Knowing that you are the emotional and physical champion of her life will intensify your love making in droves. And, the more secret the locations you chose for a quick embrace, the happier the two of you will giggle together just walking down the street.

~

Sharing Romantic Insights 2 – How we Love Together!

We're sitting on the velvety couch downstairs. We've just had a languorous bath together and we're settling in for a great 'Chick Flick' that always makes you, well, let's just say, want to cuddle extra close.

So we've turned the lights down low and nothing but the soft visuals of a naked couple together up on the screen makes us think of ourselves together on the couch. I'm trying not to be too dis-tracted because I know how you enjoy such scenes and not have me spoil the moment. But your hand begins to swirl gently around my leg. You are not quite tickling me as much as you are trying to caress the hair on my legs. With your fingertips, you know full well what that's going to do to me in less than one anticipating minute.

Still I hold on. You are even watching me grow underneath my golden red-heart silky boxers and your eyes are getting wide and anxious as it happens, for you know how well I love you once I start.

And you also know I won't let you go without a wonderful, full body kiss once I get you aroused. Your soft fingers glide up and down my thighs, the candles flutter in the darkness. You move up closer to me on the couch and put your hand tenderly on the side of my face. That is when you also snuggle one of your naked legs up over mine as we're stretched out together barely clothed.

Well, you finally get your way. I raise my chest anticipating your long, full hair waving generously across it. I slowly begin to focus on your beautiful face and body, I center on our re-actions together. I turn to you – in complete and total love – and my hands are trembling to want to touch the soft, gentle hairs along your back. I kiss your lower lip. Then we kiss fully and passionately as one. I begin to work the two of your lips between my own. Tenderly, hungrily you kiss me in return, your kisses searching my face for a spot you might not yet have loved and touched with your warm, moist mouth.

We realize that movies aren't what we want right now. You turn on the music we find so moving when we're sliding into and over and onto each other the way we're going to tonight. I am so happy to be your man, I'm so happy that you share everything with me the way you do.

I so love to taste your tummy, and your knees. I cannot believe how incredible you make me feel, how turned on I get from the simple smell of your skin and hair, the softness of your womanly mound against my cheek, the passionate sound of your voice moaning to me, calling me, and telling me you're getting close, oh so close...

And then, you take charge of our bodies. You begin to swirl up on top of me. You paint my body with your own. You raise my arms above my head, interlocking our fingers and pressing every centimeter of your skin and breasts against my chest, kissing me all the while on my face and neck. You are open for me with your long legs, and it's warm inside. You love how generously and freely I am capable of giving you everything you ask.

You quiver with every inch of me in your body, every minute of our passion, every deepest, loving sensation. You start to churn, your body's rhythm moving over me. Your eyes are shut and your mouth is open and the rushing begins to take us both. We are One Tonight!

I'm so in love with you, Sweet Baby. I want to finish our love together feeling you like never before. You can have me any way you wish and I'll hold on strong for you. Show me how this night ends, and then we'll hold each other close in our descending ecstasy and fall asleep. You can even say to me:

'Not yet mister, you still owe me more of your tantalizing kisses..., and I'm here to collect!'

Okay then, I will kiss you again, my Sweet – Just You Wait!

IStockphoto

SECRETS for WOMEN: Under the general perspectives of many men, the sweetest attribute a woman can add to a relationship is to become an unforgettable lover. Easily accomplished for most females, this is *not* normally 'a given'.

The very act of sharing minds and bodies between people in love leaves an imprint on the human subconscious that can rarely be dismissed.

And though you may not be convinced that a man is capable of such an impression, believe it when we say that if you love him with all your talents to mix tenderness and might–*he **will never forget you**.* But of course, you have to do your part. Lying there like a fluffy pillow *(or sack of potatoes)* won't always cut it.

Women have all the infinite tools they need for passion and unequivocal physical power, and so far they do pretty darn good exercising the mental half of this power as well. Yet her physical, sexually luring qualities remain relatively untapped as one of her greatest natural phenomenon.

The most fascinating female Lovers of yesterday, today, and tomorrow will never have to force their love on any man, and they know it. When a woman allows her passion to take seed in a man, she will be loved for it every time. It's the emotional connection that a man will rarely ever admit, but he constantly longs for in his search for just the right companion.

But as intimacy proceeds, there are several practical ways to keep him from exploding on you as the two of you move in and over each other with your legs, arms, and chests.

Just as he can learn to control the involuntary reactions of climaxing before he is absolutely ready – that wonderfully uncontrollable physical state of his when he's loving you – you too can learn to control the physical responses that are capable in the muscles of the vagina. Read on to discover the answers to these age-old mystiques.

Secret #1 for Her: Considering His Needs and Your Will to Improve!

Girls, becoming proficient at great, fantastic sex, we certainly hope that the results of your diligent practice arrived with as much fun attached to the experiments as the intrigue there was in doing them. As your loving abilities increase, they should distinguish you as an eager pupil in whatever talents you chose to master. Naturally, we become more prolific when the subject is something we already enjoy and have a myriad of dedicated, regular experience.

By far, one of the most enduring books on the market today for objectivity and a clear cut approach to uninhibited sex is the material outlined in the book, *The Joy of Sex, - A Gourmet Guide to Love Making*, edited by Alex Comfort, M.B., and Ph.D., published by Crown Publishers, Inc.

This sexual cookbook, along with countless others found at most book stores around the country act as a genuine stimulus to promote the fun and appreciation of good healthy intimate relations. If a problem exists that keeps a couple from exploring their physical prowess, reading books or pamphlets like this one can introduce new chapters in the appetites of hungry Lovers.

Books encourage romantic scenarios like pleasant, steamy baths, or planning dreamy getaways to faraway places like Paris or any of our great National Parks. They remind us of quiet, romantic dinners in a soft setting at home, or even a quaint Bed and Breakfast near your own home town – anything.

Thriving activities, fulfilling plans for interludes, and even toying with ideas for travel and intimacy can always strengthen the desires we have for each other. The point is to exercise new material to surprise each other on 'Date Night' or that love-binge we take when the kids are away at camp. Study love with your *significant other* with diligence, work at imaginative interludes, then get out and have some fun.

~

Poem 6. Particula Pedral. ~ Partical of Rock.

Poema de Amor #6

<u>PARTICULA PEDRAL</u>

Eres sombra de latides nacientes
púrpurn de desgarro concientes
clamor de le janas pisadas.

Tu aspereza pedral
finge dolor ante cruelec martirios
pero tu faze endurece
y ya no sientes.

Más anoñadar quisierón
en lágrimas de polvo
tu dimension fatal
no es possible.

Y del inerte crujir
de las llamaradas salientes
dolar quisiern en tupidas
raspillas tu corazón cambiar.

Ladero

Love Poem #6

PARTICLE OF ROCK

You are the shadow of nascent beats,
Purplish red of conscious tearing
Clamor of distant footsteps.

Your rocky roughness
Feints pain when faced with cruel punishment
But your face hardens
And you no longer feel.

But they wanted to overwhelm
With dusty tears
Your fatal dimension,
It is not possible.

And from the inert crackling
Of the leaping flames
They tried to convert your heart
Into countless needle sharp icicles.

Ladero
Copyright ©1997 – 2015, Juan Francisco Ladero Guevara

Secret #2 for Her: Inexorable Talents!

'The most sought-after feminine sexual response of all…' Pompoir. As one of the actual talents a woman can develop on her own was originally covered at length in a 16th Century East Indian text. Another excerpt from **The Joy of Sex** highlights this same technique as follows: *"She must… close and constrict the Yoni until it holds the Lingam as with a finger, opening and shutting at her pleasure, and finally acting as the hand of the Gopala-girl who milks the cow. This can be learned only by long practice, and especially by throwing her* will *into the part affected, even as men endeavor to sharpen their hearing. Her husband will then value her above all women, nor would he exchange her for the most beautiful queen in the Three Worlds… Among some races the constrictor vaginae muscles are abnormally developed.*

In Abyssinia, for instance, a woman can so exert them as to cause pain to a man, and, when sitting on his thighs, she can induce orgasm without moving any other part of her person. Such an artist is called by the Arabs, Kabbazah! Literally, a holder, and it is not surprising that slave dealers pay large sums for her."

What all this means is that a woman can produce one of life's greatest feelings by the pressure she can inflict on the sturdy, erect male. The actual motions and procedures involved are like this: After he's slid himself inside, a delicate timing is required during the deep, slow thrusts in and out. As he moves himself in, she relaxes the vaginal muscle network. As he draws back, she grips him firmly with her vagina. It's a gentle, subtle muscle release when he thrusts in, and then passionately out, with muscles she never knew she had, *'When he enters you, you relax, when he draws back, you grab hold.'*

Once developed and mastered, she can hold him inside her body like water is kept if she stands. Soothing, flowing, electrifying! Every touch of fingertips, every press of lips against her thighs, every move a sexy couple makes will pale in comparison to this particularly beautiful intercourse.

Ladies, this technique will have him aroused by you no matter how far you are apart, or whether it has been ten years since you've seen him last. He will never forget the ecstasy in this, and he will forever long to get it back.

After some practice, and you can actually control the pressure you exert at will, then your subconscious will take over and your rhythm will become as reflexive as breathing or blinking is to you now. You won't have to think about it, it will just be a part of you.

~

Car Wash Lovers!

Dear Babe!

Where's a simple place we can go to do our most loving, ordinary thing? Kissing. A car wash, of course! While we get all suds'd up, I can't help but think how thrilling it would be to make love with you while the windows are fogging up and the soap is lathering itself over the hood and doors. I am certainly intrigued at this intimate thought and would try to make you feel totally enriched and loved with it if I could.

So, we'd be charged and ready for each other when the tumblers rolled alongside our car, the hot foamy soap sloshing against the windows, the steamy water running down its sides, all the while we are joined as one and moving with each other to a Pandora music stream over on the radio.

It is such a joy to watch you swoon and move across my lap. But our time draws near to the end of our wash, and our mutual thrills must end as well. As the big doors open and give way to sunlight creeping through the sheen, we're suddenly in the public's eye again. Abruptly and lovingly, we appear, flustered yet totally ecstatic!

Wow, that was quick. But it was incredible too! We'll have to find another place tomorrow that lasts longer because I just can't pull off a memory like this without bringing you total satisfaction. I want to help you explode. Let's just make out until your engines are peaked and ready – again!

We are beautiful together, baby. We are good for each other. Are you really mine, my Angel!

I love you so much,
Your Hero
William J.

Secret #3 for Her: A Touch of Magic!

A Patient, Loving Grasp. Ladies! Your role in helping him control his intimate, physical response, is a pivotal aspect of his ability to improve. This should be an inherent part of every intimate setting. The idea is to grasp and hold his erection at the base of the penis. Just before he arrives at a climax, clasp the penis like a shot glass with your thumb at the vas deferens to constrict, or rather *shut off* the orgasmic impulse. Then without touching anything else or moving around in a way that could stimulate an uncontrollable release, let his urges subside.

This will help train him to "stop" when he wants to during your loving interactions. You'll be conditioning him to slow down for a moment at any time, and then continue after a moment's rest.

Your greater contribution will be from your endearing patience in all of this. As he develops his endurance for longer, more satisfying sex for you both, there will be times when things get carried away and he blasts all over everything anyway. There will be sessions when neither of you have the energy to practice; you'll just want to climb in bed together, get your *love making in for the day*, and then cuddle until you're fast and beautifully asleep.

This should occur every once in a while anyway so there isn't too much semen built up that would interfere with progress. (Otherwise, an interesting but painful phenomenon occurs. It's known as *Blue Balls* and it comes from not ejaculating over a period of many long term erections. It feels to a man, like he just got kicked between the legs!) Hello!

~

Poem 7. Alma Callada. ~ Silent Soul.

Poema de Amor #7

ALMA CALLADA

No sé si podre vivir sin tí,
me pregunto y callo

Un viento suave y frio
abraza mi cuerpo inerte
contemplo el manto oscuro
y te veo en mí.

Y veo cue eres tan alto como el cielo
que es dificil de alcanzar.

Y sé por qué, te gusta el mar,
porque es frio como tu amor,
pero aún así eres Consuelo
de mi marchito corazoñ.

No sé si podré vivir sin tí,
me pregunto y callo.

Flor de invierno,
de luz y amor fugaz.
Tan fría como mi noche,
altiva gacela.

Ladero

61

Love Poem #7

SILENT SOUL

I do not know if I will be able to live without you...
I ask myself and then turn silent

A soft and cold wind
Embraces my inert body...
I look at the dark blanket
... And I see you in me.

And I see that you are as high as the sky
That is difficult to reach.

And I know why ... you like the sea,
Because it is cold like your love,
But even that way you are the consolation
Of my wilted heart.

I do not know if I will be able to live without you,
I ask myself and then turn silent.

Winter flower,
Of sudden light and love.
As cold as my night,
Arrogant gazelle.

Ladero
Copyright ©1997 – 2015, Juan Francisco Ladero Guevara

Secret #4 for Her: Endearing Practice!

Karreza. Another interesting, easily practiced technique is additionally outlined in the book, **The Joy of Sex.** Karreza, simply put, together with the female's "**Pompoir**," describes a method of total male control that was developed by the Oneida Indians of the Iroquois Nation in upper New York. This technique calls for no male movement during intercourse, except what is only required to maintain his erection. The woman is only allowed to manipulate her body with the slow constrictive pressures described for Pompoir.

Carrying out these practices afford the two of you rewarding excitement and plenty of shuddering thrills – Microgasms, as we like to call them. Consider though, the idea here is for him to last as long as both of you desire. The point of having sex at all is the enjoyment we receive from being together in total physical bliss. And recalling the vision in the old erotic film classic, *Emmanuelle*, "It's not the orgasm my dear, it's the euphoria."

Remember as well, never take any of this too serious.
It's all about the fun, love, and companionship.

~

Passionate Letter 6. *An Afternoon of Love.*
William & Dionna: Rated Adult

An Afternoon of Love

Hi My Beautiful, Beautiful Lover,

William says, "I am sitting here blush with passion dreaming about you next to me. I think about how tender and soft you are to me when we lay next to each other, and I contemplate how wonderful we kiss together after we've spent some time apart.

I am able to talk and whisper to you in my thoughts as we melt together, so soothing. So naked.

Isn't it marvelous how our bodies remember how stirred they can get when some time has crossed between us? Isn't it interesting how responsive and quick we are to feel desire for each other and know that it's you I share my heart and body with, as it's you who shares your heart and body with me. I go days and even weeks realizing in one continuous thought that I want nothing but you at my side, and I can't do it. I feel my strong muscles flexing for you, and I feel your legs and arms wrapping around me even this far from home.

IStockphoto

When I picture love, Sweet Baby, I picture us entwined and moving slowly together in rhythm, fully and completely rocking to soft music in our ears. I feel us fully and completely touching each centimeter of our skin, so much so, that each pore is soaking up the other's love.

I adore it when your breasts swell and you grow full and hungry for my tender touch and kisses. I love watching you as I touch you with my mouth and swirl you around and around with my tender kisses, brushing you as well with my soft, full hair. As I move across your sensitive belly and slide into you 'down there', fully engulfed by your passion with me, I sweep my face against your skin because I can't hold my excitement any longer.

I need you to call out sweet words to me like you do...."

Dionna replies: *"I'm ready for you Darling, I'm so hot for you and you are making me feel so beautiful. I'm am sooooo close, and so wet. I want you to rub our chests and squeeze my body into* yours. I want you to melt all over me. I want you to kiss me between my breasts!"

William continues: "I feel you on the verge of total euphoria. I want to make out with you. I want our lips to hunger for each other's and lock perfectly together. I want to French kiss your legs, and all of you. I want you to feel my passionate kisses on and around every bit of you. I want to make you happy, and as we get to the very edge, I want to climb up your body as you are in the throes of a gigantic lift off, kissing and grasping you with my strong hands along the way, summiting to our personal peaks, rushing wildly at the very same instant!

You know how fantastic we are once I move up on you. I can grip your feet with my toes, feel your silken legs upon my legs, move your arms above your head with my strong hands and fingers, and of course touch you every place in between. We excite each other; give each other the joy of satisfying love. And for minutes after we come together, we will quiver and shutter to every delicate after-touch, finally collapsing in total fatigue and in total Love.

Yet nicely enough, while you're still soaking wet, I drop back down to kiss and cuddle you with my lips. But as we artfully let our sensitivity and tenderness subside, you like me traveling down your back and body, kissing you as I go. I find myself ultimately onto you again, tenderly swirling my kisses on top of you to the music of our bodies moving once again, rocking completely to the sounds of our own excitement.

I love you. You are so beautiful to me, Angel. Thank you for allowing me into your life. Thank you for making my world a delightful, wonderful thing."

You Are Magnificent!
W.J.

Secret #5 for Her: Inescapable Passion!

The Kiss. As men endeavor to improve their techniques with loving adventures, women should equally employ as disciplined a practice to make their kissing and passion as heartfelt and unforgettable as they can. From her perspective, if there are any barriers to making out with her man, discomforts that render her frigid to advanced suggestions in bed, it probably stems from not knowing how to kiss instead of just enjoying the act and striving to explore.

You'd be surprised at how many women neglect this simple, yet decisive talent. Clean, sweet, fresh breath is its own turn-on for a man and does more for his excitement than a quick interlude will any day.

Again, William and Dionna review a couple of the finer points of the art of the Kiss.

Dionna: When it's my turn to kiss my hero on the face, he is just that to me, My Hero! He is making me feel so beautiful with only his kiss that I can't wait to kiss him like that in return. I love to watch him as his arousal grows higher in excitement for me. When our moist, hot lips meet as one, we might flick our tongues together for a tease.

But gently, of course, after our initial beginning, we'll start to push a little closer with our tongues, reaching deep into each other's mouths. This is especially exciting for me and my loins begin to quiver as I know what's coming next – his scrumptious, luscious kisses everywhere!

William: She mirrors me when we make love. Where my chest is rising up to hers, our bodies move on top of each other in waves of cool, silky splendor. I feel her kissing every spot on me as her mouth touches down from place to place. This is when I am most emotionally tied to our love for each other.

She loves to love me orally, working me to a constant rush, and stopping short of bursting me all over. She is as tender and caring in these passionate moments as I am with her. And our love is mutual and vulnerable in these times of eager, intimate tenderness. Our love is great together and it all starts for me with her kiss.

So, take your pulsing, quivering lips, be they tender, flirty pecks on the cheeks, or swirls around your lover's face, and venture into multitudes of other sweet encouraging journeys. Making love on your partner's luscious parts help gradually increase the passions between you that no blockbuster movie star could portray.

Kissing is the very framework for how we make love with our partners. Heads, lips, ankles, knees, thighs, stomachs, ribs, and every place in between, kissing is what keeps us in love.

~

Poem 8. Pasos Acompanados. ~ Companion Steps.

Poema de Amor #8

<u>PASOS ACOMPANADOS</u>

He recorrido siglos enteos
acompañando la soledad,
en un momento le pedí
que me espere un ratito,
púes hadía encontrado en el camino,
los bellos ojos de una piedra
que por sus pupilas hilaban
cristalinas goats de bondad,
que las margaritas que la rodeaban
agradecidas le sonreian,
y la amé, la amé lo juro
como amo las cansadas manos de mi madre
quise decírselo,
más de mi salieron,
bridas de desdichas que me alban
quise decirle,
que sus dulces ojos,
supieron asir mi corazón
cuan henhebran musitadoras
mis lazos esperanzados;
la amé, la amé tanto lo juro;
y no diji nada,

Nada mis labios híbridos
y la piedra cerró los ojos,
miesntras fruncí el ceño
observando desvanecido
la amarga palabra

que me atraviesa
dolorosa

mi garganta henchida
de prosa y llanto
que gritarian cuanto la amé
Ahora, a ti piedra sepultadora
mi olor a camino soledad
me sonrien consoladora.

Ladero

Love Poem #8

<u>COMPANION STEPS</u>

I have traveled for entire centuries
Accompanying solitude...
One time I asked it
To wait a little while for me,
Because I had found along the way,
The beautiful eyes of a stone
That would thread through its pupil
Transparent drops of kindness,
That the daisies that surrounded it
Smiled in thankfulness,
And I loved her, I loved her I swear
As I love the tired hands of my mother
I tried to tell her that,
But what came out from deep inside,
Bridles of misery that praise me
I wanted to tell her,
That her sweet eyes,
Were able to capture the threads of my
Hopeful heart
Like whispering threads;
I loved her, I loved her so much, I swear;
And I said nothing,
Nothing came from my confused lips
And the rock closed its eyes,
While I frowned
Observing exhausted
The bitter word
That painfully crosses

My swollen throat
Of prose and tears...
That would scream how much I loved her
Now, you my burial tombstone,
My smell of road and solitude...
Smile at me consolingly.

Ladero
Copyright ©1997 – 2015, Juan Francisco Ladero Guevara

Photo © B.T. Dormire

- **SECRETS for You BOTH:** Companionship, patience, and like anything else in life, sharing your worlds together takes effort connecting tying the tenants of the 'Character First' qualities into your daily focus, (www.Characterfirst.com). You and your mate can apply immeasurable benefits to your physical and emotional well-being. Many of these elements include:

Contentment, Acceptance, Boldness, Thriftiness, Respect, Persuasiveness, Joyfulness, Virtue, Decisiveness, Gratefulness, Orderliness, Forgiveness, Honor, Justice, Faith, Responsibility, Initiative, Happiness, Self-Control, Pleasure, Resourcefulness, Enjoyment, Tolerance, Bliss, Creativity, Discretion, Ecstasy, Endurance, Wisdom, Benevolence, Diligence, Hospitality, Merriment, Sensitivity, Discernment, Jubilation Dependability, Availability, Security, Compassion, Truth, and Humility to name a few.

Great relationships balance knowing the list above with when to suggest passion for the night. Other times, it's good to just sit and listen to the challenges of a partner's day. Since however, *Love* is our primary focus, we'll edge toward what makes a lasting, loving standard in relationship ethics.

Arrange to hold each other together in the shower with your bodies lathered up and poised for embrace, (Candles add a nice touch with this, but don't burn the curtains.) Explore the sensations of every millimeter of contact, slowly, and deliberately. Hold yourselves while the soap lubricates you and the steam rises up between you in an exercise of sensitivity awareness.

NOT rolling over to sleep after a climax, but complimenting each other with gentle caresses and loving, verbal connections are the antidotes to a tedious monotony. Or just as nice, talk about sweet plans together, or how your days went, or if exercising together one evening during the week might be a nice prelude to a comfortable dinner out. Talk about anything, just wait the few short minutes to revive him with your caring hands, or kiss him all over with your warm, moistened lips. Should you desire, this will foreshadow even steamier responses after you both have 'recharged' for round two.

Take a deep breath and nestle down to her until she peaks. You'll soon wish you could have as great an adventure at sex as she does. And this will help you love her all the more.

Oral stimulation as foreplay. Not necessarily with the intention of taking each other to climax, but more as the seductive act of foreplay, full-body kisses are very significant. Most couples enjoy the excitement of when each relaxes into the other and just lets the gentle caresses with tongues, lips and kisses take hold. The more excited each gets, the more enjoyable the entire act of lovemaking becomes.

The skin, which is our largest stimulating playground, requires an attention on the order of patience, firmness, tenderness, togetherness, unselfishness, imagination, and any number of other observances that compliment a dedicated pair of uninhibited Lovers.

And finally...**Never underestimate the power** of sustaining the simplest of these next loving arts:*Attention, Appreciation, &Compromise.*

Attention: Remain mentally attentive to stay physically affectionate. Connect to each other by fulfilling your mental needs; when one talks, interact. Incorporate relevant dialogue and provide intriguing feedback. **Listen to each other!**

Appreciation: Bring **Her** flowers unexpectedly on a cold, gray day. Call **Him** out of the blue just to see how he's doing, slip in an occasional comment like, "Sweetheart, I'm going to kiss your face and lips when you get home tonight, and that's just for starters!" Try not to act like business partners in a relationship, but keep your identities as a couple intact.

IStockphoto

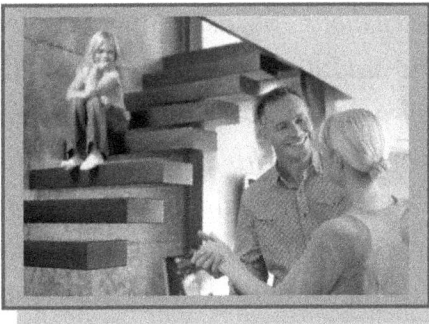

Play more with each other like the Lovers you are meant to be.

Compromise: The Art of Compromising in otherwise diffi-cult times with kids or finances are how both of you win. It gives you a chance at reconciling a loving albeit tenuous point of view.

And to clear up a sensitive, yet important aspect of our lesson here, **Children** *are what make the world go 'round*. By all means they require their own attention, but by the same token, **don't forget each other**. Not in the least. Paraphrased here for all of us to consider,

The best thing you can do for your children...

Is to love each other first!

Passionate Letter 7. *A Path to Love – Forces of Nature.*
William & Dionna: Rated Adult

A Path to Love – Forces of Nature

They kissed at last. The different flavors from the strawberries, chocolate and wine swirled together from each of their lips to the other, making their kisses even more delightful. It didn't take long for their passion to become hot and intimate with excitement. She couldn't help but bite his shoulders with animalistic fervor. She was a hungry jaguar preparing to devour her prey.

The moonlight danced on their bodies. It entered her thoughts that the forces of nature were taunting her experience. . .like the passion of the wind atop the Eiffel Tower…the sensual feeling of the warm water in the shower not long before…and now the enticement of the uninhibited embrace…these elements combined with her desires for him were bringing them to heightened, romantic places.

She hadn't noticed the sensuous music playing before now…her body on top of his undulating and relishing the moves…she always loved this pleasure from the intimate touches and motions of her Lover. He enjoyed watching her. Their bodies were moist and moved together to the crescendo of the night. He never knew how sensuous opera music could be – until being with her. She laughed sensing that after they rose to a climax, they could both go into another flurry of ecstasy without the mandatory rest in between! Not when it was this hot! He moved with her over and over again, and then…

And then...

The alarm went off and she shook herself from the dream. She watched it ringing there for a second, still mesmerized and drowsy, but thinking how real it felt just then, how beautiful it would be to have him with her at that moment. Their bodies matched so perfectly together—legs to legs, arms to arms, with tummies, chests, and lips all floating seamlessly together, all soaking each other up and thirsting for more.

She reached up and smacked down the alarming shrill, noting while she sighed, how nicely her dreams had unfurled. She sat gazing out her bedroom window wondering what he was doing right now. Was he leaping off tall buildings? Was he cooking some breakfast for another? Just how long would it be until she could see him again?

And then, there he was. She saw him parking in the street with his shinny blue Avalanche. He walked toward her door, strutting with a gallant purpose that was singularly effective in its message — "I'm going to make love to you this morning, and I am here to prove it to you!" She flew open the sliding glass door dressed only in her thin, black negligee and smiled, "You look beautiful," he said.

"I feel beautiful!" she said. "And I've been missing you, and hungry," as she engulfed him with her open, passionate kiss.

"Me too", he replied, kissing her face and holding her tightly around her bare back. "What are we going to do about it?"

"How about you come in here out of this chill and I'll fix you a breakfast you won't forget," she said.

He moaned with her. "Ummm, that sounds good, Baby. How about sharing a nice hot cocoa, or morning bath, or something else as well?"

"Can we warm our bodies first? Then maybe later we can have some have syrup and pancakes?" She wanted everything from him that beautiful morning.

Anything you want, my Heart. I am here for you and you alone." He collected her around the waist and squeezed her derriere, and he drew her into his waiting lips. She breathed in deeply and soaked up his scent and deep French kiss, longing for much more that morning than just his hands caressing her skin and her back.

There was this musical piece written for Enya's Best; quite comforting to them as they lay near the fireplace naked, with hot cocoa and their comforting refuge underneath the blanket...How sexy she looked to him as he caught a glance of her under the velvety covers. They looked beautiful together, tangled up in love.

She was pushing out her body and reaching for the stereo's remote, selecting just the right ambiance for the morning's passion to come. "Hi, beautiful," he said as he swirled down close to her and ran his hand over her legs and knees. The touch of her thighs to his fingertips built great anticipation in his heart.

Immediately she knew there was going to be the thrill of embracing love between them.

He turned her around to her stomach and started caressing the small of her back. She always loved this. As he continued up between her shoulders, kissing and brushing his hair across her body along the way, she began to swirl in excitement. Raising her head back to look, she instinctively presented her lips to his and he engulfed them with a very passionate, embracing kiss. She soaked him up within their intimacy.

He pushed her arms above her head and lay fully stretched along her back and legs. She could feel him near her, teasing and brushing her down below. She reached down and guided him with her hands, up and down along her wet and eager body, sensing how lovely and intimate they felt together. Her pleasing hips opened wider for him and he gently touched her there, slowly and deliberately moving for her with all the patience and ecstasy he could deliver.

She moaned and completely relaxed under his slow, pleasing thrusts. He felt strong sliding his body along her thighs, and back. Her hair draped over her shoulders and he smelled the fresh aroma of her softened skin. She arched her back as he reached deeper into her desire. And their rhythm was perfectly in sync together. Up and down, forward and back, all of this passion combined with their grasps of each other's legs and skin and hearts.

She was relieved to hear his voice, low and heartfelt in her ears, knowing in the few short words of sincere passion they were sharing, that there was belonging attached to them. "I Love You," he said. It was that wholesome feeling, where we know someone is there for us, without question, without doubt, and with nothing but gratitude and happiness in our hearts.

Their love that morning was sensational, the rest of the day had come as well and soon dinner was the next important goal on the list, or so she thought. In the brief period she dozed in the late afternoon, he had actually run to the local Chinese bistro and ordered up a couple of Surprise Specials and brought them back. The night was closing in and the patio awning was just waiting for them to huddle underneath for their food and close, alluring discourse.

They moved to her Jacuzzi, stepping into the heated waters un-clothed and unconcerned that anyone else might be looking on.

They sit there and enjoy the darkening sky and how the mountains begin to silhouette against the rising stars. He put his arms around her shoulders and held her smooth skin close to his. She looked up and they moved their hips to a perfect fit together as she had remembered from her dreams. He kissed her in places she hadn't felt for a long time and it sent thrilling tremors through her eager limbs.

She turned to him and brushed her chest into his strong, waiting hands. He lifted and held her up above him and kissed the bottom of her chin, then her neck, and then her red-hot lips. She pulled him closer and began to kiss his face; the feel of her arms reaching around his warm, wet back was getting her so hot. She could feel his legs too. Strong like steel between her own, they supported her as she leaned into him like the famous Rogan statue of the Nudes. She felt a pulsing in her that was rising to the surface, growing more fluid with every loving breath.

They shared each other in those early evening minutes, wishing they could hold onto the night for as long as they could. Would they stir awake again with the sunrise, intertwined together with their legs and arms and hair; their sheets a total wreck, tell-tale of the passion and care they held for each other's needs. Could they find a way to kiss again?

From William:
Hi Baby,

I love your hands. I've always thought your fingers were especially pretty. They've always looked graceful, and longing, and beautiful to me. They're the kind I'd love to feel across my arms and shoulders, just to get me started.

But I'd also like to move over your skin with my lips; from your wrists fingers, to the inside of your elbows, around your neck, and finally down your long, sweet back. I'd like to see you lying next to me and have you pull me in close, tugging on me until no light slips between our panting bodies. I want to fall asleep with you, exhausted, dreaming of our next adventure to come...

And he keeps her wanting...driving her crazy with his sensuous embraces. And oh, the way he touches her bare, smooth skin, it just sends her over the top. He touches her mouth with his lips and caresses her without reservation. She likes that. It seems that they have found their place in each other's hearts, a place worth staying. They often journey to that secret place of passion. It is the harbor where souls collide and tenderness intertwines with raw passion and wet, intimate exhaustion. And what was once perfunctory and uneasy has now become natural, real to them, and comfortable. One moment is never enough for their love. They each return to their 'place worth staying', and they love themselves together for it.

"Take Care, my Lady," he said.

Take care...W.J.

From Dionna:

Take me to Japan. Wash my back in the steamiest oriental baths; watch me move to you in the sheltered coves of their most famous spas, alluring and sensuous, telling you with one sultry, glorious look how much I love you. Tell me in return, just how beautiful I am to you again. Shower me with sunrises and fruit. Smother me in love, Baby. You are my best Love, ever! I am yours, my loving man. I will always love you with my heart and soul.

What's inspiring to me is that I really can't resist you. I want the feel of your skin on mine. I long for your manly, passionate strength pressing up against me. I want to have you day and night. I dream of us together, swaying back and forth in the most wonderful and unconventional places. I want to love you in plain sight, Baby, in danger of being discovered from others at a moment's notice. I want to meet you for lunch in a park and have the image of our impassioned silhouettes steaming up the dark glass windows of our car – at 2:00 P.M. on a sunny afternoon. I want you to lay down on me while we're parked on a roadside rest, under trees that brush a soft wind through our hair. I want you alone with me and you know it.

Everything I have is for You, My Sweetest Man.
Your Beautiful, Loving Woman...... D.J.

IStockphoto

~

E. Self-Fulfillment as a Tool – And a Relief.

Throughout history, self-gratification has stood for the solitary exercise of sexual self-fulfillment. Masturbation today helps relieve tensions in individuals who often find the pressures of everyday life relentless and unprecedented. Most of the time it provides an easy outlet to satisfy the need for sex without the help or attendance of a dedicated lover.

In some ancient cultures, and a few still sustaining these practices today, to be aroused without a climax can strengthen the libido–or sexual virility–so that when the right partner comes along, or the timing is right, the sex is much more enhanced. Some cultures, on the other hand, may consider it weak to release the loving fluids of your body without sharing it with a mate.

The contemporary outlook toward personal intimacy should focus on a little of both. Sometimes, and after a long spell without a sexual friend, it just feels right to explode with yourself for the inner gratification and relief it provides for the soul. *Sometimes we just damn well need it!*

For men: Strengthening a man's romantic capacity by raising him to the edge of orgasm without his actually having one, teaches him to control the release point by stopping and tensing the legs or abdomen. The effect of tensing the muscles of the butt or the loins instead, acts as a 'Go' signal and he can't hold back on his ejaculation.

Don't let him explode! You can keep this going for as long as you wish, but the best techniques are slow hand or vaginal movements. Mix these with kisses and wet, full-body touches and the imprint this will leave on his heart will always remain.

For Women: Some women have never learned how to experience the different types of incredible sensations their bodies can produce. Some women, when preceded by a rushing clitoral orgasm, have never experienced an immediate and momentous vaginal contraction. This can happen when her man climbs up her body after his great oral escapade, and slips inside of her, full and excited, and thrusts with her until she's totally, completely extinguished. What Queen wouldn't trade a thousand slaves for the one man who could do this to her every night of her demands? Many women have never been extended any major primordial vibrations beyond that of an infinitesimal tremor. Not many, by far, have experienced the **G-Spot** potential for getting her thunderous engines churning up to full rpm. *Going, Going, Gone!*

Tender exploration and patience in this regard can increase awareness of the ease and sensitivity she requires to reach a climax. She can also develop the ability to get better and better with the secrets we outlined before. But never trying equates to never knowing. Play with these ideas together and things will become incredible. Again, search Google for a banquet of information on the **G-spot** mystique.

Try learning about **Tantric Sex** and chakra erogenous zones. See what it takes to move a woman to her particular peak, or develop the male's erection stamina. Either solo or together, the two of you can work out a schedule to bring yourselves to the brink of euphoric collapse. By working over a period of sessions, usually only three or four, his erections will begin to last longer and longer. In return, her orgasms now, will multiply like the fruit on a tree because both of you can maintain penetration and endurance for longer than you ever could before.

One more treat to consider: **Phone-Play**. For many impassioned couples, making love over the phone can be extremely sexy, especially if you're separated over great distances or long periods of time. This also helps to teach affectionate Lovers what the other wants and needs while acting as a great turn-on from simply your mutual, intimate conversations. Though some feel that this may border on the lazier side of sexual participation, just look at it like a college sociology lab and you're learning the art of delicate, persuasive communications. Usually, the passion overtakes the lesson and you're climaxing to each other's voices anyway.

~

Poem 9. Te Encontre. ~ I Found You.

Poema de Amor #9

TE ENCONTRE

Pensé encontrarte
en tan hermoso jardín,
donde los colores y aromas
contemplando, me quedé,
tal vez con nostalgia ó alegría, mire.
El viento las movia,
como el suave trinas
de un pájaro cantor;
en el aire se confundia
el aroma fertile,
vertido por el cáliz
azul del firmamento,
donde me confundí
en los astros azules
que timidamente tiritaban,
como melodía de celeste danzar.
Pensé encontrarte
en tan hermoso sueño
y no me dí cuenta
que tus ojos negros
como faros alumbraban,
mi larga y tediosa travesía;
y no pude encontrar
tanta belleza, ni suenños
junto a la sonrisa clara
de tu sencillo mirar.

Ladero

Love Poem #9

<u>I FOUND YOU</u>

*I thought of finding you
In such a beautiful garden,
Where the colors and aromas
I remained observing,
Perhaps with nostalgia or gladness, I looked.*

*The wind would move them,
Like the gentle chirping
Of a singing bird;
In the air there was mixed
The fertile aroma,
Spilled by the chalice
Of the blue sky,
Where I intermingled with blue stars
That trembled timidly
As a melody of celestial dance.*

*I thought of finding you
In such a beautiful dream
And I did not notice
That your dark eyes*

Would light as beacons,
My long and tedious trek;
And I was not able to find
So much beauty, nor dreams
Beside the limpid smile
Of your clear look.

Ladero
Copyright ©1997 – 2015, Juan Francisco Ladero Guevara

~

F. The Discovery of More!

Be inventive in your search for healthier, more spiritually connected sexual and emotional endeavors. MSN Lifestyles or Google.com is a thriving community to find expert advice on Sexual Health related topics. Searching Tantric Sex, and Sensual Massage, 'The Liberator' pleasure furniture website, or The English Courtesan Blogspot offers variety, encouragement, and much more.

Take some Tango, Salsa, or Cha-Cha lessons and discover how charged and energetic you get from this – it's quite a workout. Get curious and spontaneous with each other again!

Explore your Lover's potential for change, or appreciate their penchant for comfortable routines. You'll be rewarded by the wonders they express in the freedoms they enjoy.

Don't 'hover' over each other. Let love transition and grow on its own accord. Feel free to enjoy every aspect of your Lover's generosity. Play unselfishly together and have fun joking and teasing each other into your respective arms ..., *and sheets!*

Love each other like there's no tomorrow!

II. BECOMING A SOCIAL VALIANT.

A. Men as Heroes.

To begin, we want to cover one important point: Some men are concerned with the probability of not being able to satisfy a dominant, more aggressive woman. But consider for example, the older generation's approach to this simple problem. Older men have little to fear that their virility will not measure up to a younger or stronger woman's appetite. These men realize that when they lie down next to a woman – any woman for that matter – that nature is going to take its course and both partners are going to have an insatiable desire for intimacy and love.

IStockphoto

Mature, consenting adults don't worry whether they can make love or not, they know that each of their sensations for physical coupling will reach the desired effect. By working on the ideas outlined in this study, Loving Couples can establish the advantage of controlling the pitch of arousal and then maintaining their sexual excitement many times longer than they ever imagined before.

So don't be too concerned, guys. If you're healthy and eager, and she wants you and you want her, when love comes calling, then your passion will always rise to the occasion, and you'll do it whenever and wherever you want it the most.

Not to be a drag, fellas, but here's Pesky Point # 1: We need to discuss a thought or two about drugs, alcohol, cigarettes, and smooth shaves? When it comes to clean, desirable, even imaginative love and companion-ship, the afore-mentioned vices or neglected conditions may discourage the promotion of healthy, lasting romance. These issues may not be the most conducive examples to lasting, memorable performances in bed.

But it only takes a little effort to be showered, shaved, and totally ready for your mate. When you walk into her candle lit bedroom with nothing on but your red and gold valentine boxers, and she knows that your heart is open for her and her alone, then that look in her eyes will be all the reward you need.

Know your partner's moods as well as their body. Know their likes and dislikes, and their fears and confidences so you can master your approach to them without unnecessary squabbling that can lead to a 'Time-out' with sexual relations. Know that she thrives on an emotional-to-physical environment – or some other relevant atmosphere that correlates directly to good, private sex.

Pesky Point # 2: Dolling out a regular gift of roses, or cooking a simple but imaginative dinner goes a very long way. Wash her car out of the blue inside and out (see auto detailing pros in your area), or pick up the house and keep it clean, or just do a bunch of other things to make her life easier and less constrained. Enticing her into positive emotions may take a series of romantic moves or gestures on your part, but do it.

Doing a little extra (visible) work around the house or with the kitchen chores, or taking a few extra minutes at 'Baby watch' during your turn may be all it takes to settle her down. Your initiative will be appreciated, and loving intimacy will be the gratitude she conveys.

Remember the great ole' edict, guys – and maybe even apply it once in a while: *What's the sexiest thing a man can do for his woman?*

The dishes!'

What's the next sexiest thing a man can do for his woman?

Just sit and listen!

Pesky Point # 3: Simply not bugging her about sex for a while may be what she needs. She doesn't always turn on to 'things' the way we do to a filled out dress atop long, tanned legs. To us, and at the end of a bad day, we may *need* a romp in the sack so we can cope with trying again for tomorrow. To a woman, asking for sex on a bad day may be an addition to carrying the weight of a ten-ton refrigerator on her back.

Women can't get into it if they're worried that the baby is going to wake up, for example, or that the car payment wasn't mailed, or she's overwhelmed with household chores (because he doesn't do any), or whatever it is with which a woman can burden herself. Life that day has to be just right for them, or they have to learn to 'Tune Out' the world as mentioned before. At least if there is going to be any intimacy attached to your lovemaking endeavors, make her feel beautiful and important, *and mean it!*

...Learn to recognize her limits and her "I can't do it every day like you" moods. Not making her out to be the villain because she says or feels like a "No!" is usually a good first step in the ongoing cycle of romantic woo's and coo's...

Oh, by the way ladies, men can have their limits too. Overdoing the 'postponement' or 'rejection' card may have his gaze straying outside the binders of love he normally has for you. Balance is the best medicine for active, healthy, romance. Just the right doses go a long way for each of you. Plan ahead and love each other madly.

~

Passionate Letter 8. *How Your Beauty Attracts Me.*
William: Rated PG-13

How Your Beauty Attracts Me

Dearest Loving Heart,
My Sweet Baby...

I often think about how beauty attracts us to its splendor. Our eyes turn toward a field of lovely flowers, spreading out for acres across a distant plain. Our breath is taken by a magnificent view brought upon us in surprise from an unsuspecting vista on a road we've never been, and our hearts soar to the crescendo of a poetic opera, calling to us through the voices of angels in the wings.

Honey, I look at you and I am spellbound. I hear your voice and I am pulled to a power that is now and always will be larger than I can ever comprehend. You are completely extraordinary to me. Your love is generous and endless in spirit, faith, and affection. You love without expecting love in return. But I know you, Sweetheart. You thrive on being loved, like I do. My soul craves romance and loyalty and protection, as does yours, Angel. I want to be the one who loves and dedicates myself to you.

I love holding you in my arms. Standing next to you so closely that we can feel our hearts beating through our chests, I feel strong again when the resonance of our love for each other melts into one, I am completed with you in every way. I am electrified by your generosity in touch, in returned affection, and in every sensation you so freely give to me whether we're alone or in a crowd of a million. But I'm afraid to keep telling you this. I'm nervous that if you hear these things from me so many times that they may wilt and fade into a cloud of routine, begging to be released as birds wishing to flee a cage to freedom and safety. But like words sitting prisoner instead, and withdrawn, nothing measures up to the real glory they hold in their potential.

I am in love with you, my Match, my Queen. My body loves loving you, my mind relishes 'mixing it up' with you – toying and playing and teasing you to your sweet laughter. My heart is ever hungry for you. I am so glad you are in my life.

Thank you, Darling, for sharing with me all our trips together. Thank you for kissing me in all the right places we have experienced, and at just the right times. Thank you for bringing me through everything and doing what you do for me.

Always love me with passion, and call me out to do the same for you. Make sure I never stop kissing you in the kitchen, in the forest on a peaceful walk, and in our entire lives as we jaunt off into beautiful sunsets.

Goodnight, My Honey.
My Naturally Magnificent Woman!
W.J.

~

B. Women as Heroines.

Of course Ladies, this goes 50/50. Keep in mind that your man can physically make love every day of his life, (relative to the fact that he usually gets excited about you once a day, if not more). If you get complacent and lose track of the last time *You* took the initiative at making love, then by all means hurdle any perceived emotional gap and improve your passion as a new priority in life.

Surprise him midweek and welcome him home from work in your sexiest, black negligee and *make* him make love to you! Purchase and **read** number-two of our suggested readings listed below,
101 Nights of Great Romance, by Laura Corn.

Naturally, the bedroom is a good place to start, but try out the kitchen table if you want, or attack him on your living room couch – or maybe visit his office during an afternoon when no one's around. Afford yourself the pleasure and fascination this can bring into your sexual focus.

"...Recall for yourself the excitement of those first romantic encounters, where we dreamed up excuses to go off somewhere and make young, vivacious love..."

Men will rarely ever say **"No"** unless they are totally exhausted, totally depressed, or totally immersed into a project where you should honor his momentum anyway. But "getting his rocks off" doesn't (necessarily) help either. Men need an emotional connection too, *though they'll rarely admit it.* Show him that there's a real desire behind your lures to make him happy.

By all means, you can always encourage and compliment his ego with comments about his love-making talents. However, if there's a problem with his performance or your emotions toward him are in doubt (often a result of the same), don't keep it to yourself. Get these barriers out in the open. In the long run, he'll appreciate and learn from his misgivings, and you will benefit from his new found efforts as well.

And Ditto: Not to be Pesky with you either, Ladies, but drugs, alcohol, or cigarettes are becoming more of a turn-off than ever these days. And not shaving your legs or underarms can have their drawbacks as well – unless, of course, you are both into the full musk-European or avant-garde 60's cultural expressions (definitely a 'don't knock it until you've tried it' thing).

But when it comes to clean, excitable companionships; and unless both of you smoke, drink, or go unshaven, these indictments to **his** desire for you may not be the most conducive to lasting, memorable sex. It only takes a little effort to be showered and have your engines freshly cleaned for your mate. You will know from his enhanced abilities to raise you to climax that your efforts have been noticed.

~

Poem 10. Nostalgia.

Poema de Amor #10

NOSTALGIA

Son peñas que al
viento lloran
mi amargura.

Cuan gaviotas sin manada en
una tarde de julio.

Ahonda sin fin mi
desespero y lagrimas que
lentamente resbalan
mi faz inerte.

Me acurruco
buscando Consuelo.

¡ No más vacío!
llora mi alma callada
termina ya nostalgia.

Ladero

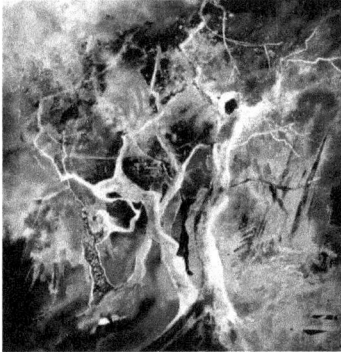

Love Poem #10

<u>NOSTALGIA</u>

They are rocks
That cry to the wind
My bitterness.

Like seagulls without companions
In an afternoon in July.

It deepens endlessly
My desperation and tears
That slowly slide
Down my inert face.

I curl up
Looking for consolation.

No more emptiness!
My soul cries silently
The nostalgia ends.

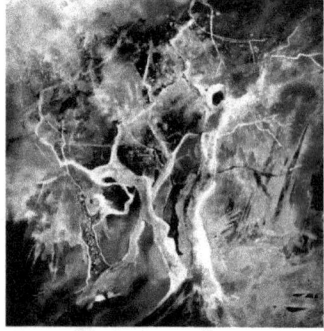

Ladero
Copyright ©1997 – 2015, Juan Francisco Ladero Guevara

C. For You Both – Champions at Heart.

Guys! Key Rule For Men – Talk to your woman! As time moves on in your life, and the routines and pressures of just getting by takes their toll on your being, pay attention to your girl and the **inner beauty she radiates for you 24 / 7.** If you ignore her or you're never home, the risk of her vulnerability to affairs from outsiders showing any romantic interest for her at all isn't beyond her reach.

However, for each of your mental and physical satisfactions, once you're under the covers, use imaginative, inspirational techniques to start kissing her from her ankles up. Make a wonderfully romantic endeavor of it. Find just the right words at just the right times. Work to make each of your lives just a little bit better each day. This is pretty much the greater focus of the entire human experience. Keep your times together close in your memory, never give up on each other. Your lives will always be enriched for it. And don't forget to vary your routine. Even your best techniques can get boring over time. Fulfill a latent fantasy every once in a while. Surprising new adventures can really be a thrill.

Keep in mind that a woman's breasts contain similar nerve and erogenous impulses as that of the male's penis. Be sure not to neglect, but also not to overuse these sensitive and important parts of a woman's body. Your desire to please her should be a lasting venture, well into giving her an erotic condition with your naked skin as you embrace yourself onto hers.

Know that you can back away from her for a moment, halting your warmest passions from an untimely flow on or between your bodies. Know that you can ask her assistance to help you hold back as well. Be aware that it takes work and discipline to benefit from all of this stamina, but you will surely be stronger for the experience.

One important point: Gentlemen, she is an electric powerhouse! Every inch of her (and you) is capable of absorbing the responsive impulse energy which is passed during sexual contact. Explore her. Move around her body, up her entire length and down her back. She will never forget you for it and will always long to be at your side.

Applaud and appreciate her worth as a human being. **Tell Her You Love Her** – regularly and sincerely. *Be a man to her!*

Have a dynamic interest in her job and work. She may be a busy housewife or a PhD in Social Psychology, but she still needs your confirmation in words *and* deeds to be able to let go of her daily pressures and tend to you in return.

~

Passionate Letter 9. *Swimming With You.*
William: Rated R

<u>Swimming With You</u>

Is There a Way to Tell You...

...*That I love you more than anyone I've ever known? That I often think about us in a faraway place, vacationing or lounging away the hours. Where the afternoon breezes are warm and inviting, and the rich Caribbean waters of our private cove are crystal blue, and tepid as a brisk summer's day.*

In the lagoon of our waters, you swim there gracefully and smoothly through the imperceptible current. You're wearing a long orange flowing skirt that's fastened only at the waist and it flows with you like a lucid, dancing scarf, blowing slowly out behind you, like the long tail of a beautiful mermaid.

But just as lucid as a woman can be, I feel you beneath me in the sheets of our cool pillowy bed. Soft and silky you are to me, my Baby, flowing, free, sliding your legs along my own, beautiful and loving and generous to me with your intimacy. And in this, you never cease to amaze me.

I'm drifting under you in our water, my Darling, watching this tranquil scene as I swim strongly with you from below. I reach up and can almost touch you, but I'm beneath you and I'm play-ing—you are titillated by the bubbles I blow up at you, swirling as they do over and around your topless body as we move, they tickle you with the softest caress.

I follow the length of you with my eyes, from your passionate toes and calves, up your powerful muscles to a place I can't see beneath the shadows, then it's all the way up to your pretty neck and ears. Oh, how I love you. I am eyeing every sensuous inch of your skin, parallel to you now, remaining upside down and looking up at how the sun brightens and shades itself through your radiant hair, billowing in golden strands behind you in the rich, blue water.

I love the way the sunlight reflects its shinning rays around you as you move your arms and legs so freely and effortlessly in the weightless sea we've found. I love the way we feel together – so luxurious when we touch each other's skin. And I love the way your full and beautiful body heaves as you use your arms to travel up through the shallows toward the glittery surface.

I rise up to meet you from underneath and I take you by your ribs in my hands as we breach our way out of the water and splash and embrace, laughing as the foamy sea washes off our shoulders and chests. I get to see only a hint of your tummy and the silhouette of your real treasure just beneath your clinging sun skirt, ocean wet against your hips and thighs.

We settle back into the soothing water wrapped in each other's arms, kissing hungrily, soaking up the salty taste of each other's lips upon the other. I love drinking you in, my Dear. I love being the Lover of your life. With you, feeling your legs intertwined with mine, silky smooth, cool and aching for every part of me to touch you, sliding, loving each other in the deep blue sea.

You love my hands holding you safely out of the ocean tide. You love leaning into my arms and you smile while I gently kiss the side of your waist and ribs and up to your neck and face

And you also smile as I brush my lips and cool, wavy hair across other parts of you floating with me in the water.

I want to bathe with you in the midnight light. I want to wash the salt and sea off of your legs and back. I want to see the soap of our shower together draining down your front, flowing between you and over your breasts and down your beautiful thighs. I want you, Baby. I want to walk with you, arm in arm. I want to sing to you, my Love.

Take me tonight, Angel. Take me into you all the way. Every inch of me is yours. Every thought I have is of you. Every breath I take I want to share with you, with your lips barely kissing mine in exquisite anticipation. I know the throbbing pulses and flooding ecstasy is going to flourish.

We collapse together in amorous bliss, sharing heartbeats with each other, laughing exhausted and out of breath, each prizing the body, spirit, and soul of the other. Each of us gladdened to have the other in our world.

We have found ourselves in the deepest of happiness, and we're swimming in love's warmest waters— – – For Keeps!

W.J.

~

Ladies! Key Rule For Women – *Talk to your man!* Carry out your romantic talents at will, but–be a woman to him. And he'll be a man for you. Keep in mind that as the routines and pressures of just getting by take their toll on your life, don't forget to pay attention to your man. You're always going to be a mother, a student, a helper, or a boss – this is a given. But be a Lover to your man as well. The risk of affairs and his vulnerability to outsiders who show a romantic interest **in the charisma he radiates** aren't out of the question.

However, remember to make loving, passionate romance with your man at least once every chance you get. If you've been together for years, love him once every couple of weeks if not more! In your advancing menopausal states, just ask your doctor for help with dryness and hot flashes. But certainly maintain or recreate your passion for witty discourse, intelligent interludes and the talks that eventually lead to spectacular intercourse with the man you love. Cherish him and don't hold yourself back. *(Remember, Sweetie, you like it too).*

Thrive with your man and have fun wherever you go. During your most treasured excitement with him, use your usual finesse and tenderness when he needs it the most – during his best, most enduring sessions with you in his arms

Dream up great places for love, and respect his attempts to please you when he hints that he would really enjoy making out on a balcony in Paris, or necking with you on a Grand Canyon overlook, or putting his hand up your back in the pasta isle at the supermarket when no one is looking. He loves you very much, so let him show it.

One important point: People thrive in social settings, especially with their significant others. Many people mistakenly feel that if their mates are engaged in conversation with someone else, that they like this better than being with them. NOT TRUE. Everyone needs to interact within their partner's social settings. At work, within their family circles, amid their most outrageous or utterly boring hobbies, throughout all their lives, men need their women, and women need their men to be integral parts of their worlds.

But sometimes it's just a 'guy's night out' thing (or vise-versa). Either way, whether you're asked to join him or not, try to go along with your partner's wishes. In settings that influence promotions, garner peer respect, or boost self-esteem, the backing of a gallant partner has long been accepted to empower a man or woman's stature beyond compare.

Ask about his day, his thoughts, or his dreams. Keep your identities close and bond with each other on a regular basis. **Tell Him You Love Him.** Get back to your cuddly, desirable roots and hold onto him until the embers in your hearts are back to a roar.

~

Sharing Romantic Insights 3 – Letter from a Lover Overseas.

Hello My Darling,

As your evening settled last night in America, I was just getting into my day – over here! I wasn't as secluded with you on the phone as I would have liked, our troops were rolling in from house to house. But if I had no crowd around me and I was truly alone, I would have embellished my love for you in poems of praise, and words of tenderness, and even a song or two about how great we are together.

If I could tell you in ten words or less that my affection for you is immeasurable, I would probably say things like, 'Your touch and love totally immerse me every day.' or, 'I won't breathe again until it's with you my Baby.' or, 'Sweetheart, we haven't made love enough this morning.' or, 'Let's walk barefoot through leaves, hand in hand in love.' or 'Can I try and repay all your kisses again today?' or, 'I could love you in a restaurant booth or airplane' or, 'With you sleeping next to me, I am totally loved.'

Or finally..., 'Can we lay together and just listen to our hearts?' and, 'I love you, today and forever, my only beautiful Darling!'

So now that I'm feeling especially romantic with you, my Honey, I'll mention that listening to you sing to me on last night's call was like smelling fresh sheets.

You were so magnificent with me that I long to be able to just hold and enjoy your body next to mine. Soon, my Baby, I will be with you again, very, very soon. In our separation, I know with all my heart that you are the most beautiful woman I have ever known, and that I love you more than any words can say. I love making love to you, I love you loving me in return.

You are magnificent and all of Paris is going to see it too when we land there and meet inside each other's arms. I respect you, Baby – Unconditionally.

And I adore you even more.

When we finally rendezvous together atop a nighttime Eiffel, I will keep you warm inside my coat, and you can move upon me if you wish, and we will hold each other close. You are very, very sexy Honey, and I just want to show you how much I care by affording you the most exciting adventures any woman ever had. You could very well say that when it comes to my loving you, Valentino, or Burton, or Fiennes are blithering hobbyists compared to the kisses you'll get from me.

You and I fit so sweetly together. We are going to rock each other so passionately on my return. I love you for your grace, I love you for your heart, I love you for your toes, and shoulders, and eyes, and nose. I love you for you, my Other'.

When I move up your sweet, smooth body from there, you will feel the rest of me as I engulf you, with silky legs, tightened thighs, heaving chests into each other, and love.

I'm yours in Life and in Romance. With you covered in Rose Petals, I have to swim through them to get to your endless and welcomed passionate ways.

I am forever speechless in your arms!

IStockphoto

III. In Retrospect –

A DEDICATION to LOVE.

Love to some people is the waterfall of life.

To others, members of the opposite sex are like paintings in a fine museum. There's a blistering, wonderful beauty around every new corner. Some people find their counterparts on this earth a living treasure, a masterful work of art, a champion of muscle, and bone, and heart.

Being with each other, enjoying, working, and harboring each other in the different places of this world, is for many of us, what it's all about. Playing sports, or traveling together, discovering mutual hobbies or new meditative experiences, all of these activities bring about a wondrous positive life. The only thing we need to do to fulfill these images is to get out and try some of them with a loving, eager partner.

You can enhance your entire quality of existence by being mindful of others and by being a realist in the world. Commit yourself to honesty and heart, feelings and intuitions. Be faithful to your Lover. Don't do things you don't want to do, but "Dare to be unique!"

Beware however, of that which comes too easy in life. You may find yourself shaken from a love that doesn't share your goals. You may have to bounce back from an unpleasant misfortune with money or a gilded romance.

Just be able to have fun and look forward to wonderful times together. At last, be able to say to yourselves once in a while what the lesson in the film **Forty Carrots** was trying to teach us about love, and passion, and life:

"I can... I will... Yes!"

Make Loving Miracles with Your Sweetheart,
Have Epic, Intimate Romances Together,
And,
Be Beautiful and Excellent to Your Partner Through all Your
Days, Weeks, and Years !!!

William & Dionna Jorgensen

The Lover's Dozen

12 Extravagant, Ongoing, Sexy Surprises!

Great Romantics in Life. . .
Come Together in the Most Interesting Ways.

You may have had one great love or many. You might fall in love with a partner you've only known for only five minutes, or one who's pampered you for fifty years. But whenever you get a chance to romance your someone special, someone who has proven that they are as honest and dear to your heart as anyone, no matter how tough the struggles were in between, then by all means, love them, or learn to love them (again if necessary) with all your mind, body, and soul.

The following twelve extravagant, ongoing sexy surprises are tenants you can use to nurture and embellish your passionate initiatives to thoroughly please your 'Significant Other'. Utilize them as they are, or feel free to spin off of their romantic intent and come up with a few exciting interludes of your own. Either way, keep your imagination on full, and your heart open to the results.

Happy Kisses Everyone!

Lover's Dozen 1. *The Sweetheart's Scavenger Hunt!*

With a little creative planning, a personal scavenger hunt can be a great surprise for someone you love. Start out with a morning card at breakfast or one delivered to their work after lunch. Aside from the usual romantic pleasantries, this is going to hurdle your partner into the hunt. "See *Instructional* text or my email to you before leaving today!"

First stop: After work, they will be heading to the best candy store in town or the nearest Victoria Secrets store. You will have the nicest box of Chocolates or maybe a new black negligee packaged up (or both!), paid for, and carded with new instructions to go to the next appointed stop.

Second stop: Your partner meets you at a new restaurant you've never been to *(okay, or an old favorite),* for an intimate, cozy dinner together – you're their waiting in advance – dressed to impress.

Stop Three: After dinner, shoo him or her off to a fine, private winery in town and have a nice, New Zealand or California Riesling or sloshy French Cab' at the ready. The card on this tantalizing element will direct the hunter to take the bottle to the last stop on the list.

Stop Four: Your mate will be heading to your home where everything is decorated with candles or ribbons, or rose pedals leading to the bedroom. You may reserve a rare Bed and Breakfast you've wanted to visit and go there instead. Hit a stylish hotel with the keys and room number already assigned where, of course…,

You will be waiting inside ready to share in the prize…
As the prize itself!

~

Poem 11. Deseo Sincero. ~ Sincere Wish.

Poema de Amor #11

DESEO SINCERO

Mi #escribir versos en cuartillas.

Pareceme monótomo,
el desear lo mejor
para tu felicidad
en la larga travesía de la vida.

Pues una vez
que tus ilusiones veas
vencida,
lucha, piensa y medita
que lo mismo hará
alguién y asi juntos
lograr la travesía.

Ladero
Copyright ©1997 – 2015, Juan Francisco Ladero Guevara

Love Poem #11

<u>SINCERE WISH</u>

My sincerity,
And my gladness seem confused,
Because today I must write
Verses in quatrain to you.

It seems monotonous,
To wish you the best
For your happiness
In the long journey of life.

Because once
You see your illusions
Defeated,
Struggle, think and meditate
That someone else
Will do likewise and thus together
You both will complete the journey.

Ladero
Copyright ©1997 – 2015, Juan Francisco Ladero Guevara

Lover's Dozen 2. Hot Lunches to Go!

Plan a special extended lunchtime treat with your lover. This should come complete with soup, sandwiches, bath, sex, catnap, and a final desert before you send them back to their day. Ooooooh, Nice.

Our suggestion is this: Make ready a peanut butter and jelly or grilled cheese on wheat bread, tomato soup with crackers, apple sauce or other delicious fruit bundle. Take a rose pedal bath or naked outside Jacuzzi, and follow it, of course, with a great afternoon of physical passion. Take a little nap to top off the event, and finally have a nice angel food cake with fresh-cut strawberries all topped with a few swirls of Hershey's chocolate syrup. *Yummy, Sexy, and Delicious!*

Then..., send their sweet cheeks back to work with the afternoon's memory etched permanently on their smile. ...*Oh yeah.*

~

Passionate Letter 10. *Our 'Together' Day.*
Dionna: Rated PG

Our 'Together' Day

Dear Miraculous!

How was our love together last night, my Hero? I hope it was as beautiful, warm, and restful to you as it was for me – either way, you deserve the best I can give you, Sweetheart. I had a good day for sure. It is so nice to know that I can hold you whenever I want. But I now await your return to me once again. I'm still waiting for your love, Honey.

Can I elaborate on how wholesome and generous your body is to mine? I want you to know how lavish and sexy you are when you walk next to me in the beachside winds. Can I say how great the shimmering moon reflects off the water and gives your arms and chest its incredible glow as we walk together along the sand? Can I tell you how much I love you today?

You are very handsome, Mister! When your body glistens in the night from lights and candles that surround our room, I get completely immersed in physical anticipation. I want us together, I want us one with each other, loving all our harnessed power so ready and willing to shake the pillars of earth when we kiss.

I get hot just thinking about how sweet our love is, and how completely open we are with each other. You make me quiver inside, Angel. You have brought love into my life and suddenly everything is beautiful to me again. Thank you, my Darling.

I was thinking about a day we could spend together. I'm not sure of the details exactly, but how about some time at home, say an all-day sensuous binge. We can play from the moment we wake up, rising to some early lovemaking and then a sweet breakfast together in bed (prepared the night before, with strawberries and yogurt, or toast and jelly, and maybe an easy omelet).

Then, maybe we can share some more loving passion together, a nice movie or two, more loving kisses together. Maybe we can do a game of Kiyosaki's Cash Flow, or Monopoly, just plain cards and Gin Rummy? If nothing else, a noonday shower or bath near the back yard pool, drying you and switching pajamas for we never have to get dressed the entire day. Let's just be sultry and loving and lazy all day... together!

That in itself comforts me more than you know. I hope it excites you too, because it certainly moves me inside to think about us thrilling each other like this for this special, extravagant 'Our Together Day'.

I Love You, Baby!
Your Dionna

~

Lover's Dozen 3. Outbound Interludes!

Our suggestion is this: Force yourselves to go one full month without making love. Then take a drive on a scenic road to a popular mountain, desert, or beachside resort. Rent a quaint, private cottage off the beaten path and fix a wonderful breakfast, lunch, or dinner for your date. Maybe do a cinnamon French toast, with chorizo and eggs, or sliced fruits.

The next event here is purely a love-making challenge. Your goal is to give each other at least two wondrous orgasms apiece throughout the duration of the day. You can shower together into a sudsy froth, hot-tub it in the open air under the stars, or lay awake in the freshness of silky sheets with your arms and legs starving for each other's touch *(completely destroying the bed while you're at it)*.

Maybe you'll want to christen the leather living room couch, or make passionate love spread across the hardwood dining room table. Knowing that your amorous spirit remains on the furniture for all future guests, gives you both a sense of mischief to remember.

After sleeping off most of the remaining visit, you can get dressed and head out to the most artistic knick-knack store in the village. Make sure it's full of candles, jewelry, and other handmade crafts of every sort. Then as a thoughtful, gesturing gift, give your beautiful Lover $100 or more to spend in that store any way they want.

~

Poem 12. A Ti Madre Siempre. ~ To You Forever, Dear Mother.

Poema de Amor #12

<u>A TI MADRE SIEMPRE</u>

*Madre hoy que tús méritos
son reconocidos y alagados por todos.*

*No te hayas en tu hogar
y los corazones extintos cansados ya,
tal vez de tu ausencia,
gritan con su silencio al viento.*

*Más luego tu renaces
y con miradn tierna y entrañable sonrisa
dejas jugar momentos de alegría
en el pensamiento de tus hijos.*

*Madre recuerdo tú lozanía
apagarse un día de junio al alborear
pero no eras tú, quien se iba
sino la figurn durmiente de tu ser.*

¡Más tu no Madre Mía!

Ladero
Copyright ©1997 – 2015, Juan Francisco Ladero Guevara

Love Poem #12

TO YOU FOREVER, DEAR MOTHER

Mother, this day when your merits
Are acknowledged and praised by all

You are no longer at your hearth
And the already exhausted hearts,
Perhaps because of your absence,
Raise their silent voices in the wind.

But then you are reborn
And with your gentle look and ineffable smile
Allow moments of joy to wander
In the thoughts of your children.

Mother, I remember your freshness
Extinguished early one day in June,
But it was not you who left,
It was the sleeping shape of your essence.

But not you, my mother!

Ladero
Copyright ©1997 – 2015, Juan Francisco Ladero Guevara

~

Lover's Dozen 4. *Always St. Valentine's Day!*

Plan the best **Valentine's Day** you can think of. Modify your romances and gestures to the levels you would if it were actually February 14th and you intended to woo and coo your lover to the highest degree. The thoughtful idea here is to vary your delivery because you will be doing this at least once a month!

Valentine's Day regulars include but certainly aren't limited to: Romantic cards, Flowers of all seasonal types, Dinners (self-cooked {with clean-up} or a good restaurant you haven't been to before), Massage in the bath or shower (possibly accentuated with a night away from the house), and finally a great evening top-off making love together until you collapse from exhaustion.

Happy Valentine's Day Forever Everybody!

~

Passionate Letter 11. *My Dear Love.*
Dionna: Rated Adult

<u>My Dear Love</u>

Dear Lover Boy,

Do you have any idea how incredible you feel beside me? The first time I felt you, it thrilled me so much. You are full, loving, and exquisite. It is so beautiful to feel you when you have gotten "excited" with my touch. We grow thrilled for each other, immersed and in love. Immediately my rich, feminine wilds that was made to take you in is stirring and aches to welcome you again.

I see us together in a large beautiful shower; black onyx tiles and gleaming brass fixtures accented by mood candles reflecting off the grand mirrors shining off our bodies. With every move we make, the perfectly warm water showers on us from all directions, running lather over and between our fit, naked bodies.

You have some sweet scented, satiny loufa in your strong hands and I thrill to your touch, Baby.

You place the body wash on my shoulders rubbing them smoothly and then from behind you gently slide your hands over and onto my perfectly rounded breasts. My body melts for you in response to the soapy feel. My hands reach back, with suds of my own as I feel your tight muscular ass, I pull you in closer to me as I press mine into you, growing more amorous as we go.

My body begins moving... I have little control. I want you to continue caressing my skin, but at the same time those places below that make me a woman, quiver in anticipation of your sweeping touches that tease me so. I soon feel your hands following the curves of my body downwards. Then I feel you sliding in from around my hips inward over my wet, satiny mound. You clean me there, between my shuddering thighs. You hold me there with gentle grasping touches wanting me fresh and ready for your sweet kisses, swirls, and tender suckling pressure. Just the thought of having you there pleases me with excitement.

I turn around into you and with the same satiny wash I slide my hands over your chest that is always so strong for me. My breasts – firm and excited – slide across your chest as I move them up and down on you. I feel my way around your sweet gluts and then I find YOU, that beautiful part that makes you my man, and I envelope you in my hands. You are hard and very full. I want to go down and kiss you fully with all my love and passion. Warm clean water rushes over our bodies rinsing us off, leaving our naked skin smooth, fresh, and anticipating our romance to come. I am kissing your lips and our bodies are so close.

You are passionate between my legs, but you have not moved into me yet. The longing is almost too much, but I am enjoying it.

I begin kissing your chest as you do my shoulders. My tongue slides down your belly as I take you in my hand and kiss you. I kiss you sweetly and gently; I take you and hear you moan in enjoyment. My hand caresses you and I sense your desire.

I am ready for you. I need you within me. Our lips are seeking each other out. Your arms and hands slide down my sides and firmly grasp my cheeks as you lift me up with strength, and purpose. I straddle you, wrapping my legs tightly around your waist and I feel you there very close. I am so turned on, and hot, and wet. You carry me to our elegant bedroom and lay me down. Can you feel how excited I am for you? With your hands I feel you searching and finding just the right spot to enter me and you know I am ready to take you in.

I feel your full hardness sliding up to me slowly and power-fully...I moan and it feels so good... so beautiful. I want to shudder with you. I want you to make me explode. I am rhythmically moving up and down with you as you cup my breasts in your hands, lifting and pushing them together as you gently 'French' kiss each excited nipple with your mouth. You look at them and admire me as I lean back to admire us together, long and slender on our blue satin sheets, gleaming in the soft dimming light. Our bodies are together as one... you are journeying into me. I like to watch us, Baby. I Love seeing you make love with me.

You look at me looking at you and we see how firm, naked, and beautiful we are together. You bend down and kiss me again, stretching, working your way over every part... Shoulders, arms, breasts, ribs, stomach. As you are doing this you reach down with each hand on my legs and passionately push my thighs wider so you can position yourself between them. You kiss each leg completely down to my ankles and up again.

You stop at my inner thighs, first the left, then the right. I want you to kiss me down there. Make out with me there, Lover. I can't wait any more.

I gently guide you onto me as I grip your hair between my fingers. I feel your lips sweetly kissing me and I can't help myself... I moan and lean back, letting you take me. I feel your tongue; your magic takes flight down there. I love the feel of your tongue between me finding just the right spots. I know I am getting wetter and more excited. You start sucking on that sensitive beacon of mine and it feels so incredible... I don't want this feeling to ever stop.

You are wonderful on me, and you slide slowly up my inner thigh and I know where you are going.... You softly find me there, kissing my heaving breasts as well, and then with flowing movements, upward with your pulsing, manly body, you begin to send me over the threshold of ecstasy.

I love you, my gallant Man.
I love you so much.... D.J.

~

Lover's Dozen 5. *Dress Up and Go!*

Make sure you're both well rested and not pressured from some daytime crisis. Be ready for the long night ahead, because one's coming tonight.

To initially prepare for this romantic endeavor, go out and have your partner's car professionally detailed – cleaned inside and out, front to back, and top to bottom. The auto detailing experts in your area really know their stuff and you'll be glad you let them do it for you.

Set reservations at a great restaurant, preferably French or Italian to set the mood, or go all out at your home for a dress-up dinner. Remember to spare no effort on the meal you prepare, but the point being to dress-up for each other wherever you wind up for food.

Next of course, is the concert, play, or opera you've hidden tickets for over the last few weeks – the thrill from your sentiment here will be more than appreciated later. Then top off the evening with a night of dancing at a place where the music is perfect. Try swing, ballroom, or even country if you're so inclined. But even your living room and a good stereo works as a worthy stand-in.

As you drive back home, put in some of your favorite romantic music. After you both have undressed each other, showered, and are in your silkiest pajamas, light the candles and break out the strawberries, cheesecake, or chocolate fondue.

Before you've even come close to finishing this delectable desert, it will be time for love!

~

Poem 13. Pobreza. ~ Poverty.

Poema de Amor #13

<u>POBREZA</u>

Palabra callada y bulliciosa,
de alegría llena y de llanto,
de lamento y de cansancio.

Quiso una vez trocarte
mi dolor saltante. Más,
todo vano asi lo fué
tú lento e inmadurable
paso asi lo impidio.

Y el dolor de los hombres
como desenterrados en abismos
lucharon por inmesurables años,
mas tu no lo entendistes

Solo de nieve supo cubrir
las crepitantes cabelleras
el intangible dolor de espera
y es aun el propósito de hombres
la endeble esperanza lo que perdura.

Eres sombra de latidos nacientes
púrpura de desgarro concientes
clamor de lejanas pisadas.

Tu aspereza pedral
finge dolor ante crueles martirios
pero tu paz es dura
y ya no sientes.

Mas anonadas quisieron
en lágrimas de polvo
tu dimensión fatal
no es posible.

Y del inerte crujir
de las llamaradas salientes
dolar quisiera en tupidas
raspadillas tu corazón cambiar.

Ladero

Love Poem #13

POVERTY

Muted and boisterous world,
Full of joy and weeping,
Mourning and weariness.

Once my burgeoning pain
Tried to change you. But
Everything was for naught as
Your slow and forever childish
Pace prevented it.

And the pain of mankind
As if drawn from the depths
Struggled for countless years,
But you did not understand.

The intangible pain of waiting was
Only able to cover with snow
The luxuriant heads of hair,
And the feeble hope is all that remains,
And is still the goal of mankind.

You are the shadow of budding heartbeats,
The purplish red of the tearing of consciousness,
The rumble of distant footsteps.

Your rocky roughness
Feints pain before cruel torment,
But your solace is hard
And you no longer feel anything.

But overwhelmed in dry tears
They tried to change your deadly nature,
Impossible.

And from the still crackling
Of leaping flames
In mourning, I want to change your heart
Into countless sharp icicles.

Ladero

~

Lover's Dozen 6. *Flowers, Flowers, and More Flowers!*

When Spring rolls around, take a day off of work and go buy live potted flowers and plant them in all the usual spots around the house. Now, place little blank greeting cards – which you're going to personalize – in several of the larger arrangements throughout the yard. Write little snippets of original poems – things that you love about your mate. Compliment their beauty and well-being again and again. Use genuine thoughts about why you fell in love with them and don't let up from the start.

When your lover gets home, have a nice dinner cooking in the stove. Greet your King or Queen warmly with kisses and hugs, then send him or her outside to collect up the cards. While they're busy at this, place rose pedals in a path leading from the door to the shower. This is where you'll have a big bow on the shower door with an invitation to come inside. You're both going to suds up now and wash each other's bodies. Caress and soothe each other in the steamy warmth, but don't explode just yet – you'll be saving that for the after-dinner desert – *You!*

~

Passionate Letter 12. *The Beachside Night.*
William: Rated R

<u>The Beachside Night!</u>

C'mon, I want you beachside!

The beach indeed, is such a solitary place when I think about it. Even with the crowds and surf splashing against the windy shore, and the great, expansive views that nudge imaginations toward the open sea, I revel in how I can strangely pinpoint my focus to examine the smallest things in you as well.

I have always liked the playful sea foam kissing the last of the sand it touches before retreating back to the reaching arms if its source.

And I've always loved the frantic little creatures digging furiously back into their murky worlds of sand and mating and lives.

But I especially love to watch our toes in the crystal warmth of the tropical water as it washes our feet and ankles free of the scratchy grains. Then I envision us lying in the gentle surf at sunset, facing each other as the warmth soothes our bodies and traces our outlines, wetting our chests together as we enjoy the talk of the coming night.

Our tropical luau is planned for some time after dark and we are growing in anticipation. We watch the hotel staff together on our blanket near the waters of the drifting tide. They light tiki lamps and set the proper mood, spreading perfect white tablecloths out for the coming guests. The final touch comes with their bouquets of orchids and coconut fruit drinks under the tall palms. I feel our night is going to be magnificent.

The waiters are dressed in white coats, purple Polynesian shirts, and black pants, and they're barefoot and handsome, a very nice touch. The waitresses have on purple blouses and white skirts, accentuating their bare brown, tropical legs and they are barefoot as well, walking through the sand. Every woman wears a lily orchid in her hair, adding soft passion to the night, and soft dreams to the hearts of their men.

IStockphoto

We look lovingly at each other and agree, it's time to get off the shore. We walk arm in arm back to our beach house and the sounds of jungle primates pierce the edge of the coming moon. Macaws, Howler Monkeys, and Cameroons screech their final pleas for some companion to join them for their night. But we are together instead, my Loving Beauty, strong and patient for the time we have ahead.

Cleansing our bodies in the soothing shower before we leave for dinner, we wash the salt and sand away from our tanned and glistening skin. And while I watch the ocean waters run off your shoulders and over your beautiful breasts, I also enjoy lathering up your entire back and rubbing the bubbles between us with my chest. From your ankles and calves, all the way up your lovely thighs and sweet round curves, I finally lather up your firm but supple arms and kiss you endlessly along the way.

It's always wonderful with body foam between us. You love how I soothe the lather into your pores with just my hands, massaging every part of you with the silky suds and fruity scents. But before we go too far, I rinse you from your pretty wet face back down to your waiting, vibrant toes. And then you do the same for me, but instead you use your hands and hair to wash my body and the soap runs down our legs, intertwined, and sensuous with each other.

I like the way your kisses taste to my lips, drowning us in the fresh and splashy water. Remember though, we have a luau to get to, so I stop you slithering against my rock hard body and step out of the wet curtain to get myself dried off, dressed – and settled down. You glance at my legs and muscular cheeks as I near the bathroom door, but I catch you staring in the mirror at me so I point to you in mischief. You smile and shake your head, 'Oh yeah', knowing that I'm going to satisfy you completely and passionately again tonight.

But how you wonder? How will I thrill you later? Will it be with fruit juices and kisses on top of your chest? A surprise massage with tropical oils and candles and me, dressed in nothing but a Caribbean sarong? Will I dovetail a tropical dinner in paradise with orchids and firelight and soulful music blending with the night? Well, you intend to find out with me soon enough, for you are going to be a passionate woman tonight as well.

And as always, a beautiful one at that!

W.J.

~

Lover's Dozen 7. *Couple's Honor Nights!*

For Him: Have your Lover invite his friends over for Monday Night Football or a monthly card game. **For Her:** Invite her friends for a Make-up or Victoria Secrets party. Then disappear to a movie or the mall for a couple of hours. Tie bows to the party favors you've arranged and placed in the fridge – beer bottles or puu-puus included. Finger paint little hearts and '*I Love You's*' in shaving cream all over your master bathroom mirror. Have snack bowls ready around the TV and card table. Have a paid-for pizza delivered – preferably by you!

Now, for the sentiment in all your preparation, slip your mate a sweet card that reads, "First party is over at 11:00 so get everybody out! The second party is private. *Be There!*" Once they're all gone, serve up some hot, juicy apple pie a la mode, a nice vanilla cappuccino, or some other delectable dessert; dressed of course in your favorite silk lingerie. Have a pleasant rest of your evening, because in words or deeds, it's going to come for you both!

~

Poem 14. Ilusion Perdida. ~ Lost Illusion.

Poema de Amor #14

ILUSION PERDIDA

Tus recuerdos inquietan mi mente,
mi tristeza inrrumpe mi pecho,
flácido y sin vida,
y un gemido rompe mi silencio.

En cada lágrima que sale de mis ojos
está una marchita ilusión
te amo y te amaré en silencio,
tu ingratitud hirió mi corazón sufrido.

Tu recuerdo será consuelo
de mi cautivo corazón
ya eres ilusión pérdida,
¿ Porque?me pregunto.

Porgue no tomarlo en serio,
si creaste en mi una pasión,
me dejaste sin vida,
y no encuentro respuesta
púes esta nostalgia me calla.

Ladero
Copyright ©1997 – 2015, Juan Francisco Ladero Guevara

Love Poem #14

LOST ILLUSION

Memories of you make my mind restless,
My sadness rushes into my chest,
Flaccid and lifeless,
And a moan disrupts my silence.

In each tear that is shed from my eyes
There is a withered illusion,
I love you and I will love you in silence,
Your other-gratefulness wounded my suffering heart.

Your memory will be the consolation
Of my imprisoned love
You are already a lost illusion.
Why? I ask myself.

Why not take it seriously?
If you created in me a passion,
You left me lifeless,
And I find no answer
Because this nostalgia silences me.

Ladero

Lover's Dozen 8. *Hearing it Makes All the Difference!*

People need to hear the words 'I Love You.' They need to be comforted by compliments, reassurances from you in person or with romantic cards, and most of all, the actual words that show how you love and care for each other.

If your partner is not as enthusiastic about your romantic advances as he or she was before, then maybe you can sit and talk about what the two of you need to keep the sparks thriving between you. This is important and both of you have to try.

Play the following word game to reinforce your mutual affecttions. Make up a list of ten sweet things you love about your mate. Now go back and forth with one loving compliment apiece followed by a tender, loving-to-passionate kiss anywhere you want. The last sweet thing you should say for each other is 'I love You, Baby', and this would be right before you melt into yourselves and the bliss of romantic tenderness. Don't patronize each other, just appreciate yourselves – You'll love the result.

~

Passionate Letter 13. *What Is Perfect?*
William: Rated Adult

What Is Perfect?

Is there such a thing…

…As the perfect smile, or the perfect look, or a perfect emotion for every occasion? Are there combinations of words, or compliments that make a person laugh or cry one of those soulful, heart wrenching laughs or cries? If I recite to you the perfect phrase or poem would your heart soar a little inside for me, or a lot? Being in love, can I whisper to you so your knees and thighs tense in anticipation of something wonderful to follow?

I think there is, my Darling. I can talk to you from a place where honesty and passion dwell constantly within my heart for you. I can murmur to you across our pillows with feeling and sincerity from deep inside my soul, the soft but transfixing words, "Let me kiss you everywhere, you sweet and beautiful woman." You'd turn to me in our bed, and without hesitation, start tasting my lips, and clacking our teeth, and swirling our tongues.

To kiss you gently on your neck or arms or shoulders is to me, the sweetest, most electrifying sensation I know. But this would not be half of what I'd say to rise you to blushing and longing for our bodies to swell and push together as one.

Ask me if I love you deeper today than I did yesterday, I will tell you that I do. Pull me into your arms and guide my kissing face to wherever you want me to go for you, and I will do this too.

IStockphoto

If I would ask you in a shopping isle at the store, "Baby, can I kiss the side of your ribs, maybe underneath your nice, loose camisole top?" Would you say yes?

You'd reply, "Not on your life, Mister! People are looking." But you'd lift your shirt a little and let me do it anyway.

I'll always ask, "Do you want my cuddles and my hair to brush across your chest with gentle teasing waves and supple, soft-borne kisses? And, may I kiss you along your curves there and other high places rising and heaving for my mouth as you grow in your excitement?"

In the candle light so beautifully shining against your body you'll tell me, "Yes, Baby, I want you to kiss me wherever you want."

And we kiss each other in heightened places and make-out together with passionate churns; our bodies weaving into wonderful sensory and intimate togetherness. I come up for air, smiling at you as you are smiling back at me...

"Honey, can I slip between you?" Maybe between your ears, or your shoulders, or your breasts, I'd think. Maybe sliding gently up and down your stomach, smoothly gliding my freshly shaven face against your skin, giving you my hard electric body along your thighs and up upon your abs?

You'll say again and again: "Slide over me, Darling. Kiss me, Honey... Kiss my arms and belly, and face. Touch my lips with yours. Smooch with me, my loving Man!"

You're so sweetly scented with your luscious body flavors. You raise your arms above your head, holding them there while I slide my fingers up your length, caressing you with my searching touch, brushing down your forearms until I cup my strong palms over your full and waiting breasts. And my arms are stretched above you too, but my body is low on you. And I breathe in the sweet air that gently breezes over your mound. I tease my face with your soft hair down there, and I tease your lovely, open legs as well with hints of little nibbles, moistened lips, and my playful, searching tongue.

"Ohhhhhhhhh that feels sooooo good...." You moan to me, biting at my wrists and upper hands still placed atop your chest. You clench your fingers in my hair, firmly holding me in just the right spot, swirling my head in the perfect rhythm with my wandering song, guiding me to apply just the right amount of pressure.

And you want me now. You want my kisses firmer and to increase in passion and placement.

You want my arms to grasp you tightly between them and you want me to enter you with the sliding aim and considerate tenderness that only I know how to do for you. We are becoming one with each other, slowly, beautifully you take every inch of me to the deepest we can lunge together. Your mouth opens hungrily for my love with you. I love thrusting in unison with you, my beautiful Woman.

I love how we move so fittingly together, minutes, and hours on end. I love your naked legs draping over my back, sliding your ankles up and down my calves, drawing me firmer into your hips, undulating in our ecstasy together, thrusting your chest into mine, inviting me to kiss your breasts and hold onto them while we move.

You look up at me with sparkling, mellow eyes and say...
"I Love you, Baby".

We lay together, exhausted and throbbing, I tell you in return,

"I love you too, Honey.

Thank You, Sweetheart. Thank You!

W.J.

~

Lover's Dozen 9. *Sunrise or Moonwalks – and You!*

With each of you in your pajamas, pick out a great spot to watch the sunrise – your yard, the neighborhood park, or some favored East-facing lover's overlook. Take along a thermos of your favorite coffee, cocoa, or lemon-honey tea. This, together with a fresh fruit ensemble, blueberry muffins, or your favorite cinnamon raisin rolls and you'll have the ingredients for a great start to your day.

You can do the same thing with a Moonwalk. Make a surprise picnic of it complete with blanket, wine, and a simple desert. Now, talk about a dreamy excursion the two of you would like to make – and be prepared to fulfill it! Plan a trip with each other and highlight the most exciting details.

Talk about saving and combining your money to afford whatever it is you hope to do. Arrange to get a jar that says *Our Journey Funds*, or *Trip Pennies*, and place as much extra savings in it that you can. Then go home and snuggle back into bed for a nice dose of good morning or nighttime loves and cuddles. But stay in each other's arms for at least an explosion or two apiece.

You know what we mean!

Who can admit they did such a wonderful thing…
To start or end their day?

~

Poema de Amor #15

MI TARDE

Mirando el horizonte gris,
sonrío....
viendo tal vez el viento
oyendo tal vez los colores
sintiendo mil te quieros, de
olvido en oscuro.

El alba se tiñe se corona
dorada
llevando el último suspiro de
mi tarde.

Los últimos destellos como
llamaradas
dibujan de rosas tus mejillas
tan lejana tras los muros
me acerco a tí,
y te acaricio,
y te beso,
y me acuerdo,
mi cariñe te acercó a mí
esta tarde,
ojala para siempre.

Ladero
Copyright ©1997 – 2015, Juan Francisco Ladero Guevara

Love Poem #15

MY EVENING

Looking at the gray horizon,
I smile…
Seeing perhaps the wind
Hearing colors perhaps
Feeling thousands of I Love You's,
Of forgetfulness in darkness.

The sunset tints Its golden crown
Taking the last sigh Of my evening.

The last glimmers
Like flames Color your
cheeks pink So far behind the walls

I come near you,
And I caress you, and I kiss you,

And I remember,
My love brought you close to me
This evening,
Perhaps forever.

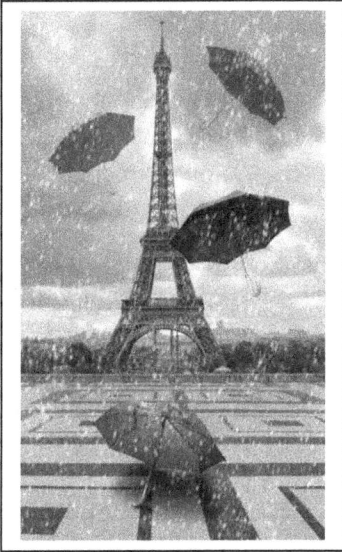

Ladero
Copyright ©1997 – 2015, Juan Francisco Ladero Guevara

Lover's Dozen 10. *Be Great Lovers First!*

Maintain your sexual playfulness in the midst of your everyday routine. Touch, caress, and hold onto each other as much as you can.

Talk like Lovers to each other every time you get a chance.

Make jokes out of the blue. Do a dazzling clean-up job around the house (or hire a maid service) so your mate doesn't have to. Cook meals in your fanciest silk skivvies. Take each other's clothes off as often as you can and hold onto or slow dance naked in front of each other more than once every blue moon.

Explore new places to make love and to eat – in fact, never restaurant out at the same place in the next ten outings. Whisper sweet nothing's to each other while people are looking at you. Ditto this loving regard especially for kissing in public places. Respect his or her notions for privacy, ever-mindful of too much PDA, but stay playful just the same.

Regularly encourage each other with sincerity and appreciation.

Compliment your partner. Care for your Sweetheart in ways *different* from everybody else. Be somebody to someone you love. And be receptive to their loving gestures for what they really are...

1. The cure for relationship doubts and afterthoughts.

And...

2. Undeniable Love!

You'll see, Baby, it pays!

~

Passionate Letter 14. *Smoothies, Trips, and Workouts.*
William: Rated PG

Smoothies, Trips, and Workouts!

Hi Beautiful.

I was thinking of something sweet to write to you just now. I know you are sleeping soundly and in luxurious comfort after our loving call together. But I would also love to have you grasp me in the night and hold me close to you as we settle back to sleep.

I relish your wonderful fruit smoothies, to mix the chilled peaches and strawberries in excitement and mischievously pour them over your ribs and other places. I think that would be fun. Of course, while keeping the sweet juices off the sheets as you jump from the chill on your body, I would have to kiss and lick you on those sensitive places in a hurry. This would be fun too.

I often think about our trip to Yosemite and the Wowona Hotel. I still have that picture of you in your long, pure white robe, standing on the banister and smiling at me, knowing that I too have nothing on but a towel. We are fun together, Sweetie. I like the thought of making love with you in foreign lands. I would love to show you many places in this world. And I will take you there as often as we can. You are passionate yet composed; fun loving and beautiful too. I can't think of any place I would want to go and not bring you along.

I want to love you on a ski trip to Whistler. I want to worry about you racing me on a mountain bike in Winter Park. Then I want to take you to our cabin for a sweet bath after our spills. Sitting in our robes, I'd doctor your skinned-up knees. I'd gladly smooth ointment over your bruises and kiss every part in between.

I would love to raise your arms above you and interlock my fingers with your feminine hands. I'd kiss you from your shoulders to your elbows, and then back to your sweet, clean ribs. It tickles you there but your reaction you bring your arms down around me and hold me close to your body for warmth and love. You gaze at me, imagining how luscious our kisses are going to be after I drink that smoothie you made with those strawberries, peaches, and your fanciful fruit ice cream.

I love your lip gloss, Honey. Every time you touch your lips to mine I taste the cherry flavors of your mouth and it lingers on with me for a while. When I taste your lips after a kiss, it makes me happy that you allow me such a gift. Thank You for that, my girl. Thank You for everything you do for me. I love you now and always, Baby.

I love you... Forever... Me!

P.S. Working out with you and sharing different exercise routines, and watching you stretch and lift and push with your legs and arms on different things is very alluring to me. And thinking or at least hoping that you are doing that for ME, makes me want to do it more for YOU as well. It makes me want to be strong and physically 'sculpted' for you. Even though I don't look or feel as perfect as most, I have more than ever, always wanted to be strong and capable for you.

But that's why I want to get stronger for you in everything I do, my mind, my body, and my soul. I want to answer your passions in the night.

I want you to use your strengths and energy to merge with mine to combine our bodies and make wondrous physical achievements together. I want to please you completely every moment we're awake.

And...I want to simply hold your hand as we walk to a Saturday matinee on Broadway in New York. I want to see you as we hike a tough Colorado trail and crest the peaks we've longed to summit, with both our legs screaming for relief, but both our legs firm and wanting more, tanned and aching for the night.

I want to be with you everywhere!

I love you for inspiring me to be more than I am.

Thank you for You!

W.J.

~

Lover's Dozen 11. *Fancy Footwork!* *(Part 1)*

You are going to do her toenails tonight, but in a very sexy way. This indeed is going to be a stay-at-home night of a beautifully unforgettable nature.

Ingredients: Candles, a fun or romantic movie (Bringing Up Baby *1938*, Shakespeare in Love *1998*, or Casablanca *1942,* for starters). Choose a nice color of nail polish that she will want to wear for a while, and gather up a soothing, favorite massage oil as well.

Prequel: Have a nice dinner and desert together under candlelight and then shower or bathe together as usual – soaping and rinsing your legs, and backs, and chests. Once you've dried each other, get into your favorite nightwear – silky boxers for him, and nothing but a sheer leopard camisole top or one of his dress shirts for her, sparsely buttoned of course.

Action: Put in the movie. He sits on the floor facing the TV and is leaning with his back against the base of a couch. She sits comfortably above him **on** the couch and drapes one or both of her bare legs over his shoulders (*so her calves rest on his chest, easily within reach of her toes from there*)...

Ahhh, to be continued....

~

Poem 16. Canto Lejano. ~ Faraway Chant.

Poema de Amor #16

CANTO LEJANO

He recorrido el contorno basto
y tibio de tu alma ensombrecida.
He pretendido incorporarte
en mi suspiro profundo y vital
en el cual tus emociones se cobijen.

Como si de un frio invierno escaparan
detrás de este pecho que se agita y soporta
un vacio sin fondo ni salida.

He escalado la barrera inútil para ver detrás
de tu mirada que se ha ido convirtiendo a
un canto lejano y sonoro
y que solo perciben los oidos afinados por el tiempo.

Ladero
Copyright ©1997 – 2015, Juan Francisco Ladero Guevara

Love Poem #16

<u>FARAWAY CHANT</u>

*I have traversed the vast
And warm contour of your darkened soul.
I have attempted to merge you
Into my deep and vital sigh
In which your emotions may find cover.*

*As if they escaped from a cold winter
Behind this chest that is restless and bears
A hollow emptiness with no way out.*

*I have climbed the useless barrier in order to see behind
Your look that has been becoming a
Faraway and loud chant
And which only ears attuned by time can hear.*

Ladero

Lover's Dozen 11. *Fancy Footwork! (Part 2)*

Speaking now for you both, and except for her sheer silk nightgown, you'll notice that she is exquisitely naked just inches from you against the back of your neck. You'll be able to caress one leg at a time with your hands and kiss her thighs lightly from side to side as you go. Take the massage oil and begin to gently rub and massage her ankles and feet, one lovely foot a time. She's going to get quite thrilled at these tender moves, and so are you.

Remove any old polish then carefully add a new color to her toes. Use some fun, foamy pedicure toe separators or Kleenex twists between them so they won't smudge. Take care, a good polish job is harder than it sounds and she still wants to look good after you're through.

While the first foot is drying, you can now turn directly around to face her and start giving her some awesome thigh kisses and stimulation. Start with her knees and thighs and move your way up! Kissing her knees, legs, and more will have her completely ready to undulate into a beautiful full-bodied thrill.

But you must stop after a few minutes and not go to the brink of a climax. Ease back down with kisses to her thighs and under her knees and then turn back around and start massaging her other leg and calf. Paint her remaining toes, kissing her shins or calves again as you go.

Modify your technique as needed for this beautiful encounter, but repeat the oral exercises for an awesome session of love until you both are smiling, exploding into each other's arms, and falling fast asleep while the movie finishes without you.

(Oh, and when your bodies are locked as one in harmonious bliss, don't forget to look back and laugh at her rainbow toe separators or cotton wads and see her cutely painted nails. Giggling together during intercourse is always a treat).

~

Passionate Letter 15. *Lady Letter Love*
Dionna: Rated R

Lady Letter Love

Aloha My Darling,

I wanted to give you a 'special good morning' note while you're there on the other side of the world since it's the start of my night over here. I wanted to say that I love and miss you very much. I am very lonely for us, Sweetheart. I'm lonely for our intimacy and our Oooh-la-la. But I also miss the loving tenderness we share from being next to you, being held in your arms and nurtured beyond compare.

This evening seems particularly quiet, Baby. I am feeling melancholy I suppose. I am going to jump in the bath now and get ready for OUR bed and wait for your call. Hurry, Honey and phone when you can, I am waiting.

Did you sleep well through your night? I think about us being together all the time. I hear songs, or see a loving or sexy commercial and think about us. I think about you in your skimpy little shorts that show without question when you are excited and that you want to come out and play.

I think about your kisses on my neck and shoulders and the hot ones on my lips. I love how you draw my lips into yours sometimes. I think about your touch from one end of my body to the other, not to mention your kisses from top to bottom and through and through!

First, I long for your touch and how you caress my body. You make me flush and ready for anything you want. Second, to have you fully excited and snuggling alongside me, that feeling is euphoric to me and I have to wrap my legs around you. Third, and best of all, I wait for your kisses on me: here, there, and everywhere. The gentle swirl of your tongue is warm and pleasing. You know how your kisses get me going and I feel myself rising with desire, wanting to feel our rushes together.

You take me sooooo far, Baby. Then just as nice, you let me subside and I feel our hearts pounding against each other. You fulfill me and I feel the passion you have for us together...I'm so turned on...I need you everywhere, completely satisfying us both over and over again.

Honey, I hope your day is beautiful. You've made mine that way and I adore you for it.

Loving you deeply as always...Your Angel

Dionna

~

Lover's Dozen 12. Dripping Wet with Water Love!

Take naked Jacuzzi's off a back porch. Shower by candlelight and baths of the same. Enjoy waterfalls in a tropical paradise splashing off each other's arms and bodies. Wade waist deep and hang on to each other in a warm secluded lagoon off a sweet Hawaiian shoreline. Lavish in the luxury of a co-ed Japanese Ryokan *(resort open-air Hot Springs)*, at sunset! All these activities are wonders you can explore whenever you desire.

IStockphoto

If you haven't bathed together for a while, then find some delicious bubble bath or shower and jump in together! Intimate Getaways are great for solitude and Love in this regard. Take time to languish in sudsy fun with your mate.

Get into enjoying the rituals of great, hot baths together. You can soap each other's backs, bodies, arms and legs. You can douse her shoulders with steamy waters like an Egyptian bathing servant would for Cleopatra. She can float over you while you're warmly underneath her and the water will tantalize your bodies for a spell.

Lying in the bubbles with her on your chest in a languorous, peaceful state is some of the best pre-bedroom foreplay, ever! When you get wet all over, you're accentuating a desire that many lovers enjoy as the optimum human experience.

Get Splashed with Somebody Today!

~

Poem 17. Ausencia. ~ Absence.

Poema de Amor #17

AUSENCIA

Esta tarde al acercarme a ti
me parecio no sentirte
tu voz sono apagada a mi oido,
tu aliento no expiraba al mio.

Tu figura yacía abstracta sin brillo
tu sonrisa, tu cuerpo, tu voz,
todo parecía ausente.

Y la tarde con su canción de agonía
reflejaba el triste amor sombrio
del alma cándida.

Ni la luz parpadeante de un astro
acudio en ayuda al lento suplicio
solo tu locuaz figura
parecía no haber sentido
el ardiento flagelo de aquella tarde.

Luego, marchamos por caminos distintos
al de antes juntos recorridos.

Ladero

Love Poem #17

ABSENCE

This evening when I came near you,
It seemed as if I could not feel you
Your voice sounded muted to my ear
Your breath did not breathe mine

Your figure lay abstract without brightness
Your smile, your body, your voice,
All seemed to be absent.

And the evening with its song of torment
Reflected the sad somber love
Of the guileless soul.

Not even the light of a flickering star
Came to help the slow torture
Only your glib figure
Seemed not to have felt
The burning flagellation of that evening.

Then, we left by different paths
From the one we had before traversed together.

Ladero

Sharing Romantic Insights 4 – When one Loves more than the Other. Or, others are Loved more than the One.

Imaginative genius and the fulfillment of physical joy,
Go together like silk sheets and love.
It is very difficult to have one without experiencing the other.

When One Loves More Than The Other...

Throughout most of this book, we've talked about how to improve our relationships, how to break new ground with our endearing equal, and how to reignite your passion-partner with heartfelt fun again. We've even addressed pleasing the one you love who is demanding and opposite from you in every way.

As *Ladero's Poem Number 17* suggests, sometimes we just can't move on with someone in our life anymore. We tire of their sass, of them chewing our ass, or their adolescent ways. The joy they once brought to us in droves is now an agonizing memory. We walk through our lives wishing the imaginary lover of our present day existence could be our long-ago partner instead.

So how do we recover from this dilemma? How do we bring our love and passion back into the fold with the person we really want?

We do it by remembering our past; our victories, challenges, and uplifting encouragements. We remind each other how important it is to overcome our differences. We hold our tempers, discuss our concerns, and readdress our mutual goals, fears, and expectations. We add to our growing history together.

We forgive our partner's indiscretions, infidelities, and indignations by somehow learning to trust again. We try to fall in love them for the heroes they were to us before. We don't give up. We move on with them, or, if we find that we really have to, we move on with someone new instead.

There is little room for in-between.

~

Passionate Letter 16. *A Last Loving Note.*
William: Rated PG

<u>A Last Loving Note</u>

I think . . .

I will write you a beautiful letter now.

As with your message to me last night while I slept, very loving and heartfelt, I will try to come close to your efforts of conveying warmth and desire into poetic, sensual, and harmonious words of love – for you.

When I think of you, Bqby, I think of trees so full that the shade casts a beautiful longing into my heart. I feel the splashing of white mist of rain as it descends onto a deep blue pond like a lover who welcomes her mate home with open arms.

When I dream of us together, we are encircled and entwined and gently floating over each other's hearts, beating and pulsing like the life in the earth, and we feel each other's skin and hear each other's whispers. I dream of our arms raised above our heads and our legs stretched all the way to our toes. And we unite with a singular purpose to please each other soooooo lovingly together. I lead us with kisses and follow each feeling's request from you for more, we hold each other tightly and warmly and lovingly until the great excitement comes.

When I see you, it takes my breath away and I know we are meant for each other in love, adventure, and challenge. I see a fit in the world like the water fits the sea, or the sun fits the day, or the passion in my heart for you fits my love. I see a great Queen and one who makes her man obey! I see me loving you for your tenderness, and also your determined strength.

I see you in a tub with Rose pedals and foamy suds, and I see me climbing in with you while you laugh and say, "Baby, you're still in your clothes." As I come up for air from our sexy, tasty kiss, with one of your shoulders in my hand and a tender but strengthened grip under you I say, "Baby, I don't have time for taking off my clothes!"

And finally, we move to our room and make love until we're exhausted, and we cling to each other all night. That is what I feel when we're together. That is what I feel right now – Impassioned, full, heartfelt love. Kissing you and making you feel wonderful all the same. Making you happy to be a Woman!

I love you Sweetheart. I always have.
I always will.
Yours in Fun and Fame,
Me!

William J...

~

William & Dionna Jorgensen

Poem 18. El Decidir. ~ The Decision.

Poema de Amor #18

<u>EL DECIDIR</u>

El estar aquí
el estar alla
me da igual.

Pues estando aquí
quiero estar alla
de estar sai.

¿ No me mueno?

Ladero
Copyright ©1997 – 2015, Juan Francisco Ladero Guevara

Love Poem #18

THE DECISION

Being here
Being there
Is all the same.

Because when I am here
I want to be over there
Being thus.

Do I move?

Ladero

<u>The Parisian Rendezvous</u>

Bon Jour Mon Amie!
<u>*From Him:*</u>

Okay, let's make it a given that both of us have been exercising and working out for months. We may not be the most sculpted bodies on earth, like those twenty-somethings at the gym, but we are incredibly eager for our ages and our lifestyles. After all, our bodies have been through a lot!

Soon, the luxury and indulgence we seek for each other arrives with our deepest love. I've called you from somewhere near India. I'm overseas coming off a climb in Nepal and I ask if you can meet me in Paris for the rest of the week.

You tell me 'Yes'. And for this I cannot wait. I'll meet you Thursday at that little cafe on Rue Tronche'. We had lunch there once. And though I've been away on my trek for 7 weeks, you want to see me there again as well.

We meet at the restaurant and give each other a marvelous French style, welcome. Even for French standards, our kiss brings smiles to the patron's watching us in envy. We spend the better part of our afternoon tootling around Norte Dame and the Basilica, but you seem anxious to get back to our room — which is now at the Four Seasons — 'George V. We stood there once watching for movie stars to appear early one evening on our first trip to this beautiful city. You were so cool that night, gazing over everyone to see if someone hot and famous was going to lunge into our midst, (Oh, that's right, we were standing there for each other all along!)

But now we're going in the front door and the Concierge with the impeccably ornate uniform welcomes us in.

As we enter the Hotel lobby, I gaze around at the extravagance of how wonderful the art and tapestries, and chandeliers and lights compliment the mass of your golden hair. You admire our brilliant reflections in the polished gold and brass of the hotel fittings and fixtures. And we are falling head over heels for each other again as you hold onto my arms and I escort you up to our room.

With our balcony overlooking a spacious Paris, we've never been this majestically romantic before. And it feels so good to be with you. You're dressed lovely tonight. You're skirt is a rustic blend of magenta lace and satin. It's kind of like a Cowgirl meets the Ballet. And it rides just below your knees. Your pale blue blouse is loose and unbuttoned a couple of extra places down from descent, but you've been teasing me now as much as you have all day.

When I sat on that bench across from the Louvre checking our map, I noticed you bending down to straighten my hair. You leaned against me in the subway and moved subtly up and down against my shirt, acting like we were the only ones in the world. And for a moment, baby, we were!

But you didn't care, you aroused me anyway.

Then your high heels entered the fray. Oh how they turn me on. Glistening red with a little strap fastened above your ankles, you walk in them like a star.

I think I want to treat you to some passionate magnificence tonight. How about a rose petal spa bath and an intimate massage?

Ever Yours,
William

To be continued....

Poem 19. La Hiedra. ~ The Ivy.

Poema de Amor #19

LA HIEDRA

Por la mañana al despertar
solía sentarme cerca al jardín
a observar el admirable empeño
de aquella hiedra.

Que, en expresíon suplicante
levantaba sus ramas, como lazos
que buscan el atrapar su presa

Y es que, aquella planta
de diminuta hoja
crecía día a día,
marcando el pasar dal tiempo.

Vencida tal vez…,
dejaba perder el aroma
de su blanca flor.

Ladero
Copyright ©1997 – 2015, Juan Francisco Ladero Guevara

Love Poem #19

THE IVY

In the morning upon waking
I used to sit near the garden
To observe the admirable effort
Of that ivy.

Which, with a pleading expression
Raised its branches, like loops
That seek to encircle their prey.

And it is, that plant
Of diminutive leaves
Growing day by day,
Marking the passage of time.

Defeated perhaps…,
It would lose the essence
Of its white flowers.

Ladero
Copyright ©1997 – 2015, Juan Francisco Ladero Guevara

~

The Parisian Rendezvous, con't:

From Her:

I love pressing myself back against you as we ride on the mirrored elevator to our room. You are delicious, smelling wonderfully like a man with only a hint of your cologne. Your strong arms are around my waist holding me tightly into you. You kiss me on the back of my neck as we wait until the older couple in front of us exit one of the other floors. They give each other a knowing glance as they walk away holding hands.

We're alone now, but we wonder to ourselves if someone else is watching. Maybe we're on camera and Times Square is podcasting us to the world. Maybe it's only because we are surrounded by mirrors and see each other from this point of view. "Look at us, Handsome." And suddenly you pull me close; kissing me passionately on my face and shoulders. Your hand reaches my back, then along my thigh…, but no! The elevator chimes like a fire alarm, telling us to stop kidding around. We've reached the Penthouse floor. Our floor, and now I'm the one dragging you toward our room.

The doors fly open and invite us into our suite, ours for the time we will share again in Paris. As we enter, you gently pull me toward you again and sweetly kiss my lips, and then you tell me you think we could use some candlelight. I agree.

While you find and light the candles, I walk over to the balcony and open the double French doors, letting in the sounds of Paris streets and stand there in awe taking in the beauty that is this marvelous city, thinking about what is to come. Just as I begin to imagine, I sense you approaching and I keep my stance…

Well now, what's coming next…?

IStockphoto

Poem 20. Beso De Mar. ~ Kiss of the Sea.

Poema de Amor #20

BESO DE MAR

¡Siempre quise escribir!
escribir hacerca del mar,
pensé que tenía la idea elara
del verde aquládo de su inmensidad.

Desde lo alto de una peña
observába como de su quituol
se tornaba en ente osco y vulgar,
golpeando alocadamente las mudas rocas sin piedad.

Y atraveq del ritino constante de su danqar
imponiá la belleqa clara de su majestuosidad.
queriendo muchas veces mostrar una fingida
apariencía de implacable temeridad.

Finalmente desnudábase su femenidad
en el tortido y diario encuentro
que sus olas sostenían con el viento.
nacía como una suave y delicada caricia
la fragante y húmeda brisa.

Ladero
Copyright ©1997 – 2015, Juan Francisco Ladero Guevara

Love Poem #20

KISS OF THE SEA

I always wanted to write!
To write about the sea,
I thought I had a clear idea
Of the bluish green of its immensity.

From the height of a rock
I would observe how its wave-breaker
Would turn into a rough and vulgar being,
Crashing madly the silent rocks without pity.

And throughout the constant rhythm of its dancing
It would impose the clear beauty of its majesty.
Trying many times to show a false appearance
Of impeccable temerity.

Finally it would undress its femininity
In the torrid and daily encounter
That its waves held with the wind.
There would be born as a soft and delicate caress
The fragrant and humid breeze.

Ladero
Copyright ©1997 – 2015, Juan Francisco Ladero Guevara

The Parisian Rendezvous, con't:

From Him:

As time goes by I realize how dynamically you've added love to my life. How you give yourself to me so unceasingly. I am in awe that you can read my very thoughts and poise yourself so beautifully at our balcony tonight. You have changed into one of my fresh long sleeve dress shirts buttoned only in the middle and you are leaning over the banister waving to young lovers in the street below. You smile and point off to the side of the ancient 18th Century architecture that makes up our life right now on the 'Au Saint Germaine.

The nicest part of this sight is your unflinching ability to share happiness with people around you. I love you for being so feminine, so much a woman at play and at heart. I love you for being my woman – and so freely immersed inside my heart!

Though you've keenly undressed and slipped into my shirt just now, I smile at where you've left your silk stockings before we went down to dinner tonight. When you said, "Oh Baby, I left something in our room. I'll just see you at the elevator in a moment." I could never have imagined that you were wonderfully smooth underneath your dressy skirt during our meal. And I probably would have never known if you hadn't asked me to rub your leg under the table because your "muscles were sore".

Sure, Honey. You giggled at my wide-eyed surprise when my hand predictably moved farther up your leg and I brushed against your body. You latched my hand between your legs with both of yours and I could see your beautifully chiseled muscles flexing to hold me there as the waiter concluded our dinner date asking if we were having dessert here or later in our room. "Thank You, Mon Signor, we will be sampling personal delicacies a bit later."

You raised your eyebrow the way you do. Ummmmm, you thought, that sounds very nice.

But sure enough, lopped over one of the ears on the porcelain, jolly-sitting elephant placed on the antique coffee table of our $850 per night French suite, were your lace trimmed silkies. It was like they were part of the very decoration this flophouse needed to spruce it up. You hung them there in honor of my faithful capacity to drape your errantly placed lingerie anywhere I want to when we're back home – the fan blade, the doorknob, the microwave handle, or any of the hundred other places I'm going to try on my return. My Motorcycle handlebars!!!

IStockphoto

But there you are, leaning on the rail of our balcony in the dark, enjoying the sequins of a million crystal lights shining out over our Paris landscape. Naturally, there is just a hint of the bottom of your cheeks sneaking out from under my shirt, falling off your shoulder to just one side.

Very sexy, Little Minx.

What's nice is that your red-strapped heels have you angled at just the right height. I place the candle on the table to add a delicate golden glow to your shinning bare legs, then tenderly walk up behind you and put my arms around your waist and share with you the fantastic evening night.

You're looking behind you and into my eyes, searching for my lips. And you find them. My kisses and desire want to search you out. They are as wet and hungry for your face as you are for mine. And something I enjoy more than anything in this world is when you and I begin to make out in these tender moments.

We kiss and swirl our lips over and around each other, and when you know you've gotten me good and completely excited, you turn back around to watch the beautiful view of lights and by chance catch a glimpse of our reflection in the side window of our suite.

And you watch me and enjoy me,
Deeply and passionately enjoying you!

~

William & Dionna Jorgensen

Poema de Amor #21

LOCURA

Mi locura es ella
que tan Linda pasea,
por los verdes pastos.

Y con blusa blonda
deja la tempestad
de su belleza

Yo, qué tán cándido
admírola y sólo
pienso en el futuro
de sus besos.

Que muerto de
ganas y ansías,
me extinto de
entre sus pasos.

Mi locura es la soledad,
los caminos y el viento
que a nosotros solos
fulgure en el silencio.

Ladero

Love Poem #21

MADNESS

She is my madness,
The beautiful one who paces
By the green pastures.

And with twill lace blouse
Leaves the tempest
Of her beauty

I, who so candidly
Admire her and think only
About the future
Of her kisses.

Who, dead with
Desire and want,
Disappear
Between her steps.

My madness is solitude,
The paths and the wind
That for us alone
Shines in silence.

Ladero
Copyright ©1997 – 2015, Juan Francisco Ladero Guevara

Passionate Letter 18. *Tropical Love.*
Dionna & William: Rated Adult

Tropical Love

From Her:

Hi, My Hot Bodied Tropical Lover,

Baby, I am thinking of you right this second. You're lying naked next to me and feeling sensuous underneath the sheets in our beachside hut. I wish I could reach out to you and rub your back and touch your firm, curvy derriere. I would slide my hand around you just to check and see if you were "awake" and raring to go!

Next, of course, I'll snuggle in close, pressing my hips and breasts upon you with a little undulating tease to get things started. By now I will have rolled over on top of you. As I sit on your abs you reach up to caress my breasts; you pull me down so that you can kiss them and snuggle both of them like you do. I feel you behind me, extremely ready. You test the "waters"... And, I play with you a little there, teasing you, welcoming you with moaning and openness, and I slide myself down on top of you... taking you all the way.

Good morning, Honey! I Love You Very Much!

From Him:

Good Morning back, My Sweet Passionate Beauty!

I have awakened to the most wonderful woman I have ever known. You are truly a fantastic partner, lover, and friend. You look so beautiful above me, moving your body over mine as we time our motions with the sway of trees in the tropical wind. You too are eager and seeking the touch of my smooth skin against your thriving treasure, taking me to every height two Lovers can reach with each other. I love you so much!

Once again I hold back with all my might! I clench your hips in my strong hands and hold you steady above me. The slightest motion is going to make me lunge all over us with excitement, and though you like it when this happens, I'm not yet finished satisfying YOU in every regard. Okay, so you like watching me erupt between our bodies, and as I love this too, things aren't going to move too fast. So, if you want to smother me with passionate kisses as we slide between ourselves, then you go right ahead. But as I said Angel, I'm going to take my time.

You are shuddering above me and I am still holding out. Finally, I slide you off of me, thanking my lucky stars I haven't peaked with you yet. I want you to share in the joy of erupting with me too, so I ease my magic back a little. You watch my moves and I give you a little eyebrow look. You tilt your head to one side and nod to me like, "Okay, Baby... Caress me again like you do. Bring me to that loving place. Make me feel like the most desired woman in your life tonight!"

My hand slides around your sweet cheeks and I feel how supple they are for me, and I run my hand up the small of your back, teasing the little hairs as I go. Then while I hold you in my arms I twirl you around and lay you down so now I am above you and strong and still excited and ready for our love.

I move slowly down your body, kissing every sweet inch from your forehead and your face, over your nose and lips and chest. I take your sweet breasts and swirl my kisses around them, bringing powerful sensations that run through both our bodies.

I love feeling them engorge again inside my gently suckling lips, cupping you in my hands, so soft yet so thrilling.

You heave your chest into me and your legs open like the blossom of a passionate rose. I can feel you wet and pulsing, shaking under me, you're so ready.

We finish our embrace and I drift into slumberous peace. You walk back into the room with a fruit smoothie in one hand and a beach towel in the other. I see that you're all dressed and ready to hit the adventure of our new day to come. Damn! What a juicy, tropical trance I was in.

'Okay then, let's go,' I think to myself. But I know what's going to happen with us when we get back to the villa later this afternoon. Do you?!

I'm going to love you all over again today, Honey. You are totally incredible to me.

Thank You for loving me so well.

~

Passionate Letter 19. *What You Are to Me.*
Dionna & William: Rated PG

<u>What You Are To Me.</u>

Hey You,

I love You...... You are fantastic...... You are loving...... You are handsome...... You are strong...... You are tender...... You are talented...... You are a great teacher...... You are an amazing friend...... You are special...... You are intelligent......You are my lover...... You are the 'bestest' ever kisser......

You are mine! I love You!   *Your Woman.*

P.S. Tonight, you're gonna get a big hug. My heart is going to open wide for you as I jump into your arms and wrap my legs around your waist, holding and kissing your magical, wonderful face.

From Him: *Hey There Back,*

You are – as always – my inspiration...... You should know that you are always in the forefront of my emotions and my love...... You are to me as endless as the wind and the sun...... You have adventure...... You have spark...... You have fear, but it guides you...... You can see that I need you and running to my side is how you respond...... You share so much of yourself with others, but most of all with me...... You don't take no for an answer when the lights go out......

And that's the best thing ever!

You long for scenic beauty, yet are most at home by a fire and a nice blanket...... You are beautiful...... You don't like scary rides, but you skydive to ease your stress...... You are honest, deserving, unbelievably passionate, and... I love you too.

When you ... Are like you are, you do these things for me and I'm amazed.

When you ... Walk into a room, I flush with all the love I've got for you, so much so, that it takes my breath away, and my soul escapes my heart.

When you ... Strut around the hanger floor—like you own the place—other people see the pride in my eyes and the swelling in my chest, and they can't help but know I love you.

When you ... Order a desert from a restaurant and say make it snappy, Jack, I hear the play in your voice and ask myself, "Who is this beautiful woman sitting next to me, and how did I come to love her so?"

When you ... Get sassy on the phone and ask me why I'm sending you love letters sketched out on a napkin in lieu of a beautiful card instead, I detect at the same time your joy and happiness as well.

When you ... Tell me you love the way I paint your toe nails after you've showered and toweled yourself dry. Tell me you are ready for the color Red, because this makes me miss you all the more.

When you ... Say you miss me, I can't help but love you more than I did the whole time before 30 seconds ago.

You are mine! And I Love You Too, Baby.   *Your Man.*

Poem 22. Epilogia. ~ Epilogue.

Poema de Amor #22

EPILOGIA

Ayer te dije que te amaba,
agache la frente y callé,
mientras oía de tus labios
setenciar mi voz con tu alma
alcé mis pupilas desconcertadas
y te sentí lejana, tan lejana.

Mientras tus ojos (los del sencillo mirar),
me golpeaban el corazón,
que se escondia en el rincón
más oscuro de mi pecho
y allí lloró, lloró sin que lo notaras,
quiero olvidarte te dije.

Pero le pedire a dios que me ayude
por que solo no podré
tal como puso en mis ojos
tus pasos y tu sonrisas
igual borre tus huellas
que me dejastes en el alma.

Ladero

Love Poem #22

<u>EPILOGUE</u>

Yesterday I told you that I loved you,
I bowed down my head and kept silent,
While I heard from your lips,
Sentencing my voice with your soul,
I raised my eyes confused
And I felt you far, so far.

While your eyes (those of the clear look),
Beat my heart,
Which would hide in the
Darkest corner of my chest
And there it cried, it cried without you noticing it,
I want to forget you, I told you.

But I will ask God to help me
Because by myself I will not be able to,
Just as he put in my eyes
Your steps and your smiles
The same way God erases the marks
That you left in my soul.

Ladero
Copyright ©1997 – 2015, Juan Francisco Ladero Guevara

While Being Apart...

Hey

I miss you very much, but that's a good thing and it will be a sweet, sweet reunion when we get to be together again!

I can't help but think about us and what I'd say if someone asked, "Give me a reason to believe in your attraction."

I'd say......

I'm attracted to my beloved Darling because she is a full-blown woman. She is spitfire and vinegar, and she has a way about her that thrills me to my soul. When I watch her walk she swaggers a good Hale Barry in a cat suit and she isn't the hootier for the effort. She just struts her stuff and that's the way it is. But when it happens, the whole earth shakes for me inside and I want to scream to everyone in earshot, "I love this woman!"

I'm especially attracted to her because when she dresses, oh man! She dresses like a Fox! She can Cha-cha a pair of high heels like no movie star ever could. She can complement an evening dress with legs to stop a room full of romantics. And her figure is unbelievable, she has a body like a show dancer, but she's always been like that – saucy and huggable, and in just the right places. She is a total woman; beautiful, loving, and tender in every regard. She's vulnerable, passionate, sometimes mysterious, quite often mischievous, and a total cutie to boot!

This girl is hot and beautiful and I would never change a hair on her head. She may not be perfect sometimes, but she's my vision of imperfection and I'll hold onto that image of our lives together forever and a day.

I can think of a million other things to validate my love for her, like how she might look in a tub full of bubbles and rose pedals, with the sweetest scented candles all a glow. Like how the light shimmers off of her golden shoulders and how her hair floats over her rising chest when she knows I'm coming near.

IStockphoto

Or how I'm so attracted to someone I can talk to so freely, who loves me as much as I do her, who believes I'm as tight a match in mind, body, and spirit as I also do for her as well.

She thinks about me and feels a quenching desire inside that even when we're apart, I can make her tremble imagining our legs together, or our arms stretched around each other, or clenching our fingers together in full and intimate moves as we glide along each other's skin. These are things I think about with my Woman.

I'm attracted to my Sweet Lover because when she smiles, the world receives a glimpse of what heaven is really all about. Her lips pucker up when we joke about something sexy, like she's gritting her teeth and about to chomp on me—so I better watch it—and I do. I also try to kiss her mouth back into juicy connection and it always envelops mine in perfect form and I love her for it.

And that is what I'd say to someone who asks my reason for loving her.

I'm in love with this beauty again today, my Beauty, and I'm in love to stay.

As Always,
Me !!!

~

Poema de Amor #23 – Ecos, Echoes

<u>ECOS</u>

Escucho ecos pedazos de mi Corazon dejado atras
Ecos de emocionces que no puedo borrar
Un imagen que consume mi mundo de memorias de tu precencia
que solamente me dejas solo
Ha tratado tan fuerte de no dejar mi soledad continual en un es-
pacio abierto tu me ayuda consiguel la luz y atraerme a un lugar
major

Pero aqui estoy luchando en esta carretera con desiciones que
tengo que decedir una manera o otra
Escojo un camino y no importa si estoy bien o mal
Pero estoy parado en la puerta para entrar a un dominio Nuevo o
a regresar a algo igual Una decision se va ser
No puedo escapar las desiciones que siempre esta ahi para mi

Espero un largo tiempo para la verdad en mi en ese hombre frio
que nunca tengo que depender de alguien
La persona que llora en secreto y que no comparte su dolor la
alegria que esta cerado tan ondo y en su major esta tan frio
Estos ecos no se quieren ir

Tengo que ir atras a ese lugar que no sabia que el Corazon me tra-
iciona llevandome a un lugar que no quero ir
Porfavor dios ayudame encontrarme

Todavia estoy viendo tu ojos que me atrajo
Todavia escucho la voz que me unde
Todavia siento tu manos que me proteje
Todavia siento tu presiencia que me calma

Lloro que quien me va a limpia mis lagrimas
Grito y quien va a espantar la noche
Persigo todo en mi y espero los ecos en mi Corazon para siguir el
camino

B. T. Dormire

Poem of Love #23 – Echoes

<u>ECHOES</u>

I hear the echoes, pieces of my heart left behind.
Echoes of emotions that time cannot erase.
A loving image engulfs my world with memories of your presence
that only leaves me brooding, or alone.
I've tried so hard not to let my loneliness draw me into a
continuous spiraling rift. You help me seek the light and draw me
to a better place.

And yet here I am on this narrow road battling the decision one
way or the other.
I blindly choose a path, neither way apparently right nor wrong.
But I'm standing at the door to enter a new domain or to return
to that which is so familiar. A decision will be made.
I can't escape the choices that are always there before me.

I long for the return of my truest self in that cold familiar man
who needs to turn to no one.
The return of this person who cries in secret and does not share
the pain, the joy, or the desire that is locked so deep, is still so
distant at best.
These echoes don't seem to leave.
I have to go back to that self who did not know that the heart
betrays, taking me places it shouldn't go.
Please God, help me find that self.

I still see your eyes that drew me in.
I still hear your voice that floods me.
I still feel your hands protecting me.
I still sense your presence that calms me.
I weep but who will wipe away the tears?
I scream but who will chase away the night?
I search for all of me and wait
For the echoes in my heart to lead the way.

Byron T. Dormire
Copyright ©1997 – 2015, Byron T.Dormire

Passionate Letter 21. *A Final Tender Massage.*
William: Rated R

A Final Tender Massage

My Dearest Sweetest You,

We have just come off the beach and it is dusk outside. We've been playing all day in the sun and swimming–a lot! I finally coax you out of the water where you'd love to stay – but you look at me and know it's time to clean off in our villa overlook by the sea.

Our bath tonight is exquisite and you languor in the suds and refreshing steam. I sit on the side with just a towel, cupping fresh hot water over your shoulders and back and front. Because you are so tired you get out and barely dry off. You just plop face down on the bed completely relaxed, and completely without any of your clothes, not even a towel to cover up the nicest part of your back – beautifully round, passionately inviting curves, calling out to me, "My Love, I want your hands and kisses to start their work on my legs tonight."

I can't imagine not touching you everywhere, but I wait and make sure the candles are lit and placed just right. The balcony windows are wide open to our veranda and only the sounds from the sea trickle through to entice our ears and our senses in the coming night.

I have the massage oil and I'm rubbing and lubricating my hands with it as I watch you in the golden wave of flickering light, radiating your body resting so peacefully there. It feels nice and cool to you as I touch you above your ankles and gently start to move in tiny circles with my firm, lubricated caresses up your calves. You enjoy my massaging the oil up your legs in little drips of warmth.

I do my best to comfort your feet in warmed lotion and I move to kiss you behind your lovely knees.

I add more care to your legs and my hands feel so natural on them. You really enjoy me giving you a great thigh rubdown as you can feel me brushing closer to you and up your back. And every so often, you feel ME caressing your calf with sensations rising up your body and you begin to want much more than the little nibbles I've only thus produced.

I splash some coconut oil on my chest, enough to lubricate us both and I now lay upon your lovely back. You moan and start a little swirl under me and you feel so moist against my skin. You rise up on your elbows and search out my mouth with yours. I love kissing you from behind as we seem to hunger for each other's lips. I brush your hair off your shoulders and begin to kiss and fondle the center of your back and around your neck.

I reach under and grasp your body in my hands. You want me to caress you with my oily palms. I rub them in swirls and gently touch everything about you that is hot and ready for more. You raise yourself in the air a little for me. I reach down and gently melt within you, my body full and flexed finding just the right place to swoon with you under me and we're both in total pleasure, bonding together as one.

Of course, I'm so ready to express my love for you by exploding between our bodies. But I wait! You turn over and I hold your shoulders with my palms, then I spread your arms above you as we slide fully along each other, inch by inch, kissing, smelling, and loving this so much. And this is when I start to lower myself down your body, brushing my hair over you and touching your sides.

Then my face rests upon you, Honey. I move between your knees and taunt you on your upper thighs with my teeth. You rise up and provide the perfect place for me to engulf you.

With my teasing lips and mouth, I love kissing you, Baby. I'm your prisoner and have to make out with you and explore every inch and side and depth of your very being.

You pull at me, unable to restrain yourself from wanting more. You pull on my hair and guide me to your heaving, beautiful chest. I have tickled your legs with my fullness, playing between your thighs and you grab me and guide me toward you. You want me close to you, full and rewarding. And I want to please the entire length of you from head to toe, helping your excitement. Making you glad to be a woman and in my arms tonight.

We have ourselves on the brink of mutual splendor. I can feel you gaining momentum and your legs begin to crush me. You are letting go of everything, letting the rush come in to your stomach and thighs, and then you pulsate and start to move. And since we're so close, I move back down on you and my touches are pleasing through and through, and we gently swirl together in unison. You are feeling perfectly loved by me, over and over again.

Our kisses work their magic, your body trembles in one electric motion and you crave me at your side and want to bring me to your special heights. You draw me up to where we can make out and move together as one. I gently kiss your breasts on my way to your mouth while we unite with the fullness of the greatest Lovers.

We undulate in perfect rises and descents together, and we roll in timely, perfect unison. And now, as we've laid skin-to-skin again so sweetly tonight, we start to erupt in each other's arms. Great euphoric waves sweep over us and we begin to rush completely and simultaneously with each other at last!!!!

We exist completely in a hot, passionate embrace; loving our bodies and our souls together as we so nicely do. Throbbing and throbbing in our intimate union.

We sense our chests crossing and touching each other to enhance even more of our euphoria together, with your embraces so strong and passionate and my whole being seeking your comfort and protection.

I love you sooooo much, my Darling. I love you from the bottom of my heart. You do these things to me and every day I dream more and more about our lives together.

We lay exhausted, shivering with every final touch. We want to fall fast asleep now, holding on tightly throughout the night.

Thank You My Sweet Angel. Thank you for being so good to me.

I love you now and always.

Your Strong and Grateful Knight!

W.J.

~

To this point, we conclude our loving advice, our Great Letters of Passion collection, and Juan Ladero's, Poemas De Amor, *Poems of Love!* We hope you've enjoyed this aspect of our interactive, romantic condition, and pass the readings on to someone wonderful in your life. We hope you share them with someone you Love.

But most of all, wherever True Love takes you in your journey to become an intimate, loving companion, be sure to enjoy each other to your utmost content!

You Absolutely Deserve It!

To suggest that we continually examine our ties to one another, is both a classic and a venerable understatement. Once you channel your sights and charisma to focus on one special love, **Lasting Intimate Secrets** reiterates that we idolize these partners and stay the course of imaginative, compelling romance.

Sustaining our loving, pampering adoration for each other is the primary, everlasting success – **no matter what!**

We encourage you to further your journey of Romantic Study and stop by **BlueSunRomance.com**.

Travel this day's dream,
Grateful that one more is here,
Love always lingers.

. . . Dormire

Live Well...Laugh Often...Never Love Enough!

Suggested Readings /Contemporary Reviews / Webs:

1. The Joy of Sex, - A Gourmet Guide to Love Making, 30th Anniversary Edition, edited by Alex Comfort, M.B., and Ph.D., published by Crown Publishers, Inc.

2. 101 Nights of Great Romance, by Laura Corn, published by Park Avenue Publishing.

3. 101 Nights of Great Sex, by Laura Corn, published by Park Avenue Publishing.

4. The Art of Tantric Sex, by Nitya Lacroix, published by DK Publishing.

5. Erotic Massage, by Anne Hooper (and any other book in her series), also by DK publishing.

6. Mars & Venus in the Bedroom, by John Gray, PhD, published by Harper Torch Publishers, an imprint of Harper Collins Publishing.

7. The Complete Kama Sutra, translated by Alain Danielou, published by Inner Traditions International, Limited.

8. A dozen Movie classics: the best Romantic Movies of all time, opinion commentary by Howard Creech. www.Google.com : Keyword – Best Romantic Movies

9. Lovin' For Life, 365 Easy Ways to Show you Care, and other works by Lisa J. Peck, www.RedemptiveCommunity.com/site/ store/

10. Adam & Eve Novelty Online Store, www.adameve.com

11. Sex Health Advice – www.goaskalice.columbia.edu

12. Google, Bing, Yahoo, and many other Search Engines – www. Goggle.com , etc.

13. Enhanced Sensual Photography – www.obsessionart.com

14. Romantic Relationship Growth through Fun, Love, Travel, and Understanding! – www.bluesunromance.com

Always Enjoy that Special Person in Your Life.

~